AGENTS UNKNOWN

AGENTS UNKNOWN

TRUE STORIES OF LIFE AS A SPECIAL AGENT
IN THE DIPLOMATIC SECURITY SERVICE

CODY J. PERRON

Agents Unknown
True Stories of Life as a Special Agent in the Diplomatic Security Service
Copyright © 2018 by Cody J. Perron
All rights reserved.

No part of this book may be reproduced in any form without permission in writing from the author.

The opinions and characterizations in this piece are those of the author and do not necessarily represent the U.S government. It is an unofficial book and not a U.S. Department of State product. Mentions of names, organizations, and places associated with U.S. Department of State are not intended in any way to infringe on any existing copyrights or registered trademarks but are used in context for educational purposes.

The author is no longer currently affiliated with, or representatives of, the specific department, organizations, or authorities in this book. The facts, opinions, and statements expressed in this book are solely those of the author and those quoted and do not reflect the opinions and policies of the U.S. Department of State. While every precaution has been taken in the preparation of this book, neither the author nor the publisher assumes responsibility for errors or omissions.

Cover photo by Cody J. Perron
Cover design by JustYourType.biz
Interior design by JustYourType.biz

ISBN-13: 978-1985818941

Contact: cody.perron@gmail.com
Follow Cody J. Perron on Instagram at @agentsunknown
and @codyp_socal

To Mom and Dad.

TABLE OF CONTENTS

v |	Dedication
ix |	Preface
xv |	Prologue
xix |	Acronyms
1 |	Chapter 1 Rookies
13 |	Chapter 2 Operation Wrecked Safari
33 |	Chapter 3 Bombs Over Biden
47 |	Chapter 4 Spartan 26
69 |	Chapter 5 A Million Dollar Fraud
85 |	Chapter 6 "Ben" There, Arrested That
103 |	Chapter 7 Firing Minh
121 |	Chapter 8 A Bad Day
139 |	Chapter 9 ISIS At The Gates
159 |	Chapter 10 Because of Delal
171 |	Chapter 11 You Don't Want This
183 |	Chapter 12 Duck and Cover
203 |	Conclusion
211 |	Bibliography
215 |	About the Author

PREFACE

Many years ago, when my mother told me I should write a book about my work and world travels as a special agent with the Diplomatic Security Service (DSS), I thought to myself, "Why would I? I've done nothing special." So many thousands of agents had come before me, and they didn't write a book. Who would be interested in reading my story? Mom even got me a journal, you know, the kind you write in with a pen. I never used it. I was too cool for that. Of course, that was 2009. I was a new agent, and I just didn't have the time for it.

Until now, I never thought I'd write a book. But, as I've resigned, nine years after first joining the DSS, nostalgia is setting in. I regret not writing in that journal and logging the experiences in over forty countries and multiple U.S. states. Fortunately, I've told these same stories many times over which have helped me to vividly remember the events depicted in this book.

The Diplomatic Security Service (DSS) is the law enforcement and security arm of the United States Department of State. It is a global force of U.S. special agents serving in over 175 countries, making DSS the most widely represented U.S. federal law enforcement agency in the world.

The DSS mission is to provide a safe and secure environment for the conduct of United States diplomacy. That sounds like a very broad set of duties, and that's because it is. DS special agents, commonly referred to as DS agents, have numerous global responsibilities that are often atypical of a special agent in the federal government.

Overseas DS agents duties include protecting U.S. diplomatic facilities, U.S. diplomats, and sensitive information. We accomplish this by managing a myriad of security programs to include United States Marine Security Guard detachments, local guard forces, physical, technical, and procedural security programs, liaison with the local government security apparatus and more.

DS agents overseas also conduct criminal, counter-terrorism, and counterintelligence investigations, often times in collaboration with other U.S. federal agencies and foreign law enforcement entities. DS agents also locate and return most wanted international fugitives from around the globe. [1]

In this overseas capacity, special agents with the DSS hold the title Regional Security Officer or RSO. The Senior RSO at every U.S. Embassy, Consulate, or Mission is the lead law enforcement agent and security advisor to the ambassador, the U.S. President's direct representative.

DS agents protect the United States Secretary of State. The Secretary of State's protection detail, commonly referred to as the Secretary's Detail or SD, travels the world conducting close protection for the appointed Secretary. DS agents in field offices around the U.S. augment those details by traveling in advance to set up security before the Secretary's arrival.

Although security and law enforcement experts, DS agents are also diplomats when serving overseas. We are highly trained and well-educated global citizens. In order to become a DS agent one must possess a bachelor's degree, be 21

---

[1] "Bureau of Diplomatic Security," https://www.state.gov/m/ds/.

years of age, and be able to pass a background investigation in order to receive a top secret clearance. To be competitive, one should possess an advanced degree, have military or law enforcement experience, or language capabilities. In general, the hiring panel wants candidates with "real world" experience from an array of professional backgrounds. DS agents are military veterans, accountants, business people, teachers, and police officers. We come from across the United States and from all walks of life.

DS agent candidates endure approximately seven months of Basic Special Agent training: first at the Federal Law Enforcement Training Center (FLETC) in Glynco, Georgia, and then at the DS training facility in Dunn Loring, VA. Before going to an overseas assignment, DS agents must complete three months of additional training in security management. In addition to the basic and security management training, if a DS agent is assigned to a high-threat assignment such as Iraq, Afghanistan, Pakistan, Yemen, and more, we then receive 3–4 more months of tactical training. At many overseas assignments, language training is required. DS agents could spend from six months to one year in language training. Much of this training has to be repeated every five years.

The DSS as an organization is relatively anonymous. As a federal law enforcement entity, most people don't even know it exists. The Rock, who plays a badass DS agent in the Fast and Furious franchise, is perpetually dodging bullets and kicking ass. And while most DS agents don't have the biceps or glistening smile of Agent Hobbs, but we do get to kick a little bit of ass of our own on occasion. Overshadowed by FBI agents and mistaken for Secret Service agents, DS agents sacrifice their lives daily in some of the most arduous environments around the world. We do more work with less resources, and we do it better. Most of what DS agents do goes unseen, unheard, and unknown, thus the title of this book "Agents Unknown."

The DSS history speaks for itself. DS agents have put their lives on the line in support of diplomacy for over a century. We were in Tehran when the U.S. Embassy was overrun by a hostile mob of college students in 1979. We were protecting the embassy in Beijing during the crackdown on protesters at Tiananmen Square in 1989. We were at the U.S. Embassies in Dar Es Salaam and Nairobi during the 1998 bombings, when Osama Bin Laden first made his mark. We were in Benghazi, Libya, when the U.S. facility was attacked on September 11, 2012. DS agents have died in service on Pan Am Flight 103 over Lockerbie, Scotland. They have died in their bunk while sleeping, and in motorcades protecting diplomats in Iraq. DS agents have been at the forefront of American diplomacy, bravely protecting those who advance American interests around the world.

Unfortunately, if the American public does hear about the DSS, it is because of some type of failure. Too often when a catastrophic event occurs at an overseas U.S. diplomatic facility, I see some hired "analyst" on national news attempting to speak intelligently about embassy security operations. Oftentimes, it is a former high-level military official or former FBI agent. Wrong dudes, CNN. If you want to know how the U.S. government protects its diplomatic personnel overseas, look to a DS special agent.

In this book you will be reading stories of my personal experiences as a DS agent. The stories will give the reader a more comprehensive understanding of the issues DS agents face and who we are. The book's intent is to be an easy read of short stories, told from my perspective, truthfully and candidly. I wrote this book on my own, utilizing the most effective Cajun grammar, and Marine lingo as possible. These stories are meant to make light of serious situations, make fun of already humorous situations, and for the DS agent reading it, to nod their head in agreement.

As you proceed through the chapters, anyone who is mentioned in full has given me their permission. I have utilized pseudonyms for active special agents and alternate names for some organizations in an attempt to protect their identity. Lastly, nothing in this book is classified. I know because I lived it and wrote the reports. If you feel something is left out or not explained in as much detail as you would like, that is because out of an abundance of caution, I decided to leave out any information that is sensitive.

In this book you'll note chapters of excitement, danger, and, chaos. But you'll also read about impactful human issues such as bullying, accidental deaths, internal stugles, and more. This is the life of a DS agent. It's not always glamorous, but it is always real.

Finally, this book is dedicated to the special people in my life. In particular my mother, Gwen, and father, Mike: two of the most selfless parents any son could ask for. I left them twenty years ago to start a life of my own. They've worried about me—not knowing where my next adventure might be. This book will shed some light on that. I miss you both immensely and am happy that I can now share more time with you each year. This book is also dedicated to my big brother,

Blake, and my big sister, Dana. I often regret I wasn't there to be the Uncle C I could have been in person to your children. I will be around more often now and hope that they know they can rely on me for anything. To my gorgeous fiancé, Krystine, you have changed my world in so many ways. I am grateful for every minute I get to spend with you. Thank you for putting up with me throughout this book writing journey. Lastly, to Balyn, my Chere Baby, the most adorable four year old around, I hope someday when you are older, much older, you will give this a read and be proud of your "Daddy Big Guy."

   Thanks, y'all. Enjoy.

PROLOGUE

"Ali! Tell this muther fucker to slow down! I didn't come to Iraq to die in a fucking taxi!" I yelled to the U.S. Consulate's Cultural Advisor. Ali, a U.S. Army Intelligence Analyst, and I had just landed in a helicopter on a Peshmerga military base in Dohuk, Iraq. Dohuk is located in Northern Iraq, about 75 kilometers north of Mosul, the ISIS stronghold, and about 65 kilometers east of the Syrian border. Upon landing, I learned that this was no regular base. It was a parking lot on a hill protected by one dude with an AK-47. From that parking lot, there was a barely paved winding road leading down the hill, which at the bottom, I soon discovered, was only guarded by a drop-arm "gate." Who needs security? It's only Iraq.

The driver was allegedly a Peshmerga military officer, but I wasn't so sure. He was wearing civilian clothes, had a robust belly, and a big Saddam-like mustache: typical of Iraqi men. He was driving like a maniac, didn't speak a lick of English, and clearly couldn't read non-verbal cues as my hand began turning purple while clutching the "oh shit" handle above the passenger side door. The taxi ride was set up by the intel analyst, but he had only been in country a few days. He worked with the special operations guys, and I trusted those dudes, but none of them were with me. My only backup was Ali, who was unarmed, and this analyst who a week prior was working a desk job in Washington, D.C.

Earlier that October morning in 2014 when I departed from the "Old Terminal" at the Erbil International Airport, I had little information on what I was getting myself into. I knew I was going to interview a teenage girl who had been held hostage by ISIS and that U.S. special operations forces offered to give us a ride in one of their helicopters. I was dropped off with Ali by two of our Personnel Security Specialists, or PSS, who worked at the U.S. Consulate. I was armed with my Glock-17 9mm pistol, three magazines filled with ammunition, and a PRC-17 multi-band radio. I had a "go bag" with medical supplies, a map of northern Iraq, "chem lights," two cans of "smoke," some protein bars, and 500 U.S. dollars hidden on me. The special ops boys didn't allow us State Department types to bring our rifles on board their helicopter, so I made do with what I had.

I walked up and down the sidewalk at the terminal trying to find a gate to get inside. I made a call to the intel analyst who said something like "find the rusty gate." "A rusty fucking gate?" I said to Ali. "Is that some kind of code?" After a few minutes of searching I finally found the gate and was granted entry. Behind it, in this dilapidated terminal was some of the U.S. military's most sophisticated equipment: tac'd out little bird helicopters, gnarly fixed wing aircraft, and the U.S. Special Operations most formidable ninja-troop carrying vehicle—the Toyota Hilux. As Ali and I entered the gate, we went left passing all of the special operations toys on our way to the tarmac.

As I approached the tarmac, I saw what appeared to be a cargo helicopter painted baby blue and white—the colors of the

United Nations. I can only assume those colors were painted on the helicopter to appear non-threatening or as a neutral force. The State Department tried that tactic in Baghdad as well. I entered the helicopter and I noticed that the inside had been stripped out and replaced with some advanced munitions. The crew was made up of a couple dudes wearing civilian clothes manning the guns and the pilots. They greeted me as I came on board. "Have a seat, sir, and buckle up," one of the men told me. He handed me a headset with a microphone.

The guys flying and manning this helo were from the U.S. military's special operations command. These dudes were highly trained, experienced, and revered in the military community. I had the fortunate opportunity to serve as liaison to special operations during my time in Erbil. They were there to conduct some serious missions, primarily "HVT," or High Value Target, operations. We were lucky to get a lift from them.

So how did I get on the back of this very sophisticated helicopter with these special ops cats? Earlier in the week, the U.S. Consulate in Erbil had received a phone call from a United Nations Refugee Camp on the Iraq-Syrian border. They stated that a young Yazidi girl, a religious sect located primarily in northern Iraq, arrived to the refugee camp over a week before. After interviewing her, they learned she had some information that the United States Government (USG) would undoubtedly be interested in. The girl, fifteen years of age, escaped the grasps of ISIS: The Islamic State of Iraq and Syria. She and her friend found a way to the border and ended up in the refugee camp.

The information obtained from the girl was forwarded to the RSO and tasked to me. One of my duties at the consulate as an ARSO was "Personnel Recovery." In a nutshell, personnel recovery duties are to liaison with all available USG assets in order to facilitate the successful recovery of isolated Americans in northern Iraq. In this particular instance, I was tasked to gather more information by interviewing this Yazidi girl and report back my findings.

The information relayed to me from the United Nations was that this girl was held hostage by ISIS with two other people she thought were Americans. One, we later learned, was from New Zealand. The other was described as an American lady with shoulder length brown hair, fair skin, and only spoke English. She was from Arizona and had a tattoo on her rib cage of a feather. She was kidnapped in Syria after crossing the border from Turkey.

The information sounded authentic. I needed to confirm so I contacted FBI Legal Attaché in Erbil, Matt. Matt took the information and ran it through their missing persons databases. A couple of hours later, I received a call. "Cody, it's Matt. This looks legit. Where can we meet?" Because the only classified space was our antiquated Tactical Operations Center (TOC), which was about the size of a walk-in closet, I decided we'd meet in my office. Matt arrived within minutes.

"What you got, Matt?" I asked.

Matt began, "Our databases show that the FBI is searching for a girl who disappeared in Syria. She was living in Turkey, crossed the border to Syria and vanished. She fits the description of the girl you describe. She has been missing since last year."

"Ok, so who is it?" I asked.

"Her name is Kayla Mueller."

ACRONYMS

ACOG - Advanced Combat Optical Gunsight

AIC - Agent in Charge

ACS - American Citizens Services

AED - Automatic External Defibrillator

APD - Ambassadors Protection Detail

ARSO - Assistant Regional Security Officer

BIAP - Baghdad International Airport

BFT - Blue Force Tracker

CBP - Customs and Border Protection

CCC - Consulate Community Center

CDO - Career Development Officer

CFI - Criminal Fraud Investigations

CG- Consul General

CODEL - Congressional Delegation

COM - Chief of Mission

C-RAM - Counter-Rocket, Artillery, Mortar

CSH - Combat Support Hospital

DBFTF - Document Benefit Fraud Task Force

DEA - Drug Enforcement Administration

DPO - Deputy Principal Officer

DS - Diplomatic Security

DSS - Diplomatic Security Service

DRSO - Deputy Regional Security Officer

ECM - Electronic Countermeasures

ERT - Emergency Response Team

FBI - Federal Bureau of Investigation

HFO - Houston Field Office

HIRRT - Helicopter Insertion Rapid Response Team

HPD - Houston Police Department

HQ - Headquarters

HRM - Human Resources Manager

IA - Iraqi Army

IBM - Iranian Backed Militia

ICE - Immigrations and Customs Enforcement

IDF - Indirect Fire

IED - Improvised Explosive Device

INP - Iraqi National Police
IP - Iraqi Police
IPD - Independent Protection Details
ISIS - Islamic State of Iraq and Syria
ISU - Iraq Support Unit
IZ - International Zone
LGF - Local Guard Force
LZ - Landing Zone
MLAT - Mutual Legal Assistance Treaty
MOFA - Ministry of Foreign Affairs
MPS - Ministry of Public Security
NEC - New Embassy Compound
NIV - Non Immigrant Visa
OMS - Office Management Specialist
OSCI - Office of Security Cooperation - Iraq
OSHA - Occupational Safety and Health Association
PAX - Passengers
PIP - Performance Improvement Plan
PL - Protective Liaison
POC - Point of Contact
POD - Protective Operations Division

POW/MIA - Prisoner of War/ Missing in Action
PPE - Personal Protective Equipment
PPS - Personal Protective Specialist
PSD - Protective Security Detail
QRF - Quick Reaction Force
RSO - Regional Security Officer
SAW - Squad Automatic Weapon
SecState - U.S. Secretary of State
SD Team - Surveillance Detection Team
SDA - Staff Diplomatic Apartments
TC - Triple Canopy
TDY - Temporary Duty Assignment
TOC - Tactical Operations Center
UNHCR - United Nations High Commission for Refugees
USSS - U.S. Secret Service
USG - United States Government
USMIL - United States Military
VBIED - Vehicle Borne Improvised Explosive Device
VP - Vice President
VPOTUS - Vice President of the United States

Chapter 1

ROOKIES

In mid-April of 2009, I sat in a large conference room on the 23rd floor of the DS Houston Field Office (HFO) in downtown Houston. In the conference room with me were my two Basic Special Agent Course classmates, Dirk and Audrey. We were waiting for our supervisor to arrive to give us a brief about HFO policies and procedures.

After waiting for approximately fifteen minutes, a short man with a stone face and balding head walked in at the other end of the conference room. He looked as if something were bothering him. He proceeded forward to the head of the table where Dirk, Audrey, and I were waiting. I stood to shake his hand, but he just looked me in the eyes and walked past, ignoring my gesture.

John was his name.

"You're going to be assigned vehicles. Don't fuck up in these vehicles. Don't drink in these vehicles, and don't take them to run your personal errands. I don't need anyone up my ass because you fucked around in these vehicles. Understood?"

he asked as he looked at the three of us. We all nodded and said, "yes, sir." John got up and walked out. "Good start," I said to Dirk.

After our meeting we were given a tour of the office and assigned to our cubicles where we completed our check-in documentation. All three of us assigned to John's unit were given cubicles right outside his door. There was a reason for that. Seniority rules and those who had been in the office longer than us took the opportunity to move as far away from John as possible. John wasn't a bad guy exactly; he was just misunderstood initially. I learned that shit talking and dropping "F-bombs" were one way to gain his approval. No problem, I got that.

After a week in the office, Dirk and I decided to "run a lead." A lead is preliminary information about a case that needs to be developed further. This lead in particular was at an elderly lady's home. It was Dirk's first case, and I was there to assist. Dirk's intent was to gain information on the elderly lady's maid who he was investigating for federal passport fraud.

Dirk and I knocked on the door and began working with our newly developed skill set. "Hello, Mrs. ... We're agents with the U.S. State Department," said Dirk as we identified ourselves with credentials and badges. "We are hoping to ask you some questions about your maid, Maria. She's not in any trouble or anything, but we just want to verify some details." So charmed, the lady let us in.

We entered the very large two-story home, and the first thing we noticed was the amount of mounted big-game trophy animals that were hanging from the wall. From the looks of it, the lady or her husband were exotic game hunters. Dirk, a hunter himself, was enamored with the trophies.

"Wow, what a collection you have! Are you a hunter?"

"No, my husband is. He frequently goes to Africa for hunts."

I could see Dirk's face light up. Noting some of the items around the room and commenting on them in an attempt to build a rapport was part of our training. This is done so that the person being interviewed begins to let their guard down. Dirk continued to discuss the animals at length, probably for about fifteen minutes. He was on it. Maybe a little too much.

After a lengthy discussion about hunting, Dirk finally proceeded with the task at hand. He asked questions: Does Maria still work for you? When was the last time you saw her? How does she get back and forth to work? Do you have any contact information for her? So on and so forth. The lady answered the questions with ease. She claimed that she did not know most of the answers to those questions. Dirk and I accepted that answer at face value. Rookies. We ended the interview after about twenty minutes and were on our way.

As we walked back to the car, silence filled the air. Dirk and I, being brand-new naive agents, were thinking, "Wow, what a nice and honest lady." Then Dirk broke the silence.

"Hey, man. Did we just get worked over by an 80-year-old lady?"

"Yeah, we did."

"Shit, let's get out of here."

Dirk and I had a good laugh and then sped out of there embarrassed at our performance. Looking back, we're confident the lady played us. We left that home with zero information of value. We reported to John, "She had nothing, boss. On to the next lead."

In DS we don't have partners as some local police departments do, but because Dirk and I were such good friends, we worked together quite often. Dirk and I fed off of each other. He was slow and methodical; I was fast and aggressive. He was the turtle, and I was the hare. Dirk became very good at investigations and was selected to head up the newly created DS position with Immigrations and Customs Enforcement (ICE) Document Benefit Fraud Task Force (DBFTF).

Some months after the Dirk and old lady debacle, I was finally about to make my first arrest. I was investigating a man named Demetrius. Demetrius was a 6'3" tall and 290-lb. man with an extensive criminal record. He had been previously arrested on aggravated battery charges, assault on a law enforcement officer, grand theft auto, and more. I was investigating him because he was utilizing fictitious information to obtain a U.S. passport. The social security number he provided on the U.S. passport application did not belong to him, he misspelled his name, and there appeared to be some possible forgery of the details on his birth record.

I investigated Demetrius for months before obtaining an arrest warrant from a federal judge. I conducted surveillance, interviews of former employers, and even former girlfriends. This guy was a scam artist. He used variations of his name, social security number, and date of birth for multiple employers. Even his girlfriends knew him as a different name.

During one of the surveillance operations, I recall the garage door opening, and I noticed a car inside. I took notes of the license plates and ran them through the DS Command Center. The plates came back to a Hertz Rent-A-Car. It was reported as stolen. I called Hertz and learned that Demetrius rented it and never brought it back. That was good news for us. The local police would definitely want in on this arrest and to recover the stolen vehicle. That was our final surveillance operation. The next step was to get the warrant.

A couple weeks later, I drafted an affidavit of probable cause and submitted it to a federal magistrate judge. After the judge signed it, I briefed the team on the arrest operation, and then we made our way to arrest Demetrius. The team drove from Houston in separate vehicles heading north to Plano, TX.

During my surveillance operation, I was able to get a floor plan of Demetrius's apartment from the leasing office. The leasing agents were full of good intelligence about Demetrius. Demetrius lived with his brother, and they were often heard arguing. The leasing agents also told us that Demetrius was not on the lease, and they asked him to leave on several occasions. They even warned the brother that he would be evicted if Demetrius didn't move out. Still, he remained. Demetrius was often volatile with the ladies at the leasing office. They were scared of him.

I learned that Demetrius's brother generally left for work around 0800. We wanted to hit the house with only Demetrius inside. Less people means less threats. We set up surveillance on the house around 0630. Soon 0800 came around, and there was no movement. The brother did not leave. 0830, still nothing. I called the leasing agent to see if she had more information. She reiterated that the brother usually leaves around 0800. 0900 rolled around and I informed my new supervisor Patrick, of the situation over the radio.

"Boss, leasing office says he usually leaves at 0800—If he hasn't left by now, I don't think he is going to leave."

"Roger that, Cody. Do you wanna hit it?"

"Yeah, let's do it. On me, let's roll up and stack on the door."

Our team of six DS agents and four local police officers were spread out among the perimeter of the home. We had determined that the far side door would be our entrypoint because there were windows that looked out among the main door. The entry team was made up of only DS agents. The four uniformed police officers remained on the perimeter watching the other doors along with the one DS agent from the Dallas office.

As I moved my car to block his garage, the rest of the team moved in. We all exited the vehicles, silently made our approach to the door, and lined up in our stack to make entry. I banged on the door and yelled, "Police with a warrant; open the door." I kept banging aggressively. "Police with a warrant; open the door!" We heard nothing inside. "Breacher up!" I yelled. One of the guys came over with the "ram," a rubber and metal fabricated device created for law enforcement to smash through doors on just this type of occasion. As the agent reared back the ram, we heard on the radio, "He's running out the back door!" Shit! The stack moved around the back side of the house.

When I rounded the side of the house, I saw the local police officer stand-up wrestling with Demetrius and trying to get him to the ground. Patrick tackled Demetrius low, and I hit him high. It felt like I was in a football game and sacking an overweight quarterback. As we wrestled him to the ground, we yelled, "let me see your hands; keep your hands out of your pocket!" We rolled him to his stomach, and I put my knee down on his ear.

"It hurts," he screamed.

"Stop resisting!" I shouted.

Patrick was around his waist and noticed that Demetrius's shorts were falling off exposing his ass-crack. "Pick up your pants!" Patrick shouted as he grabbed his shorts by the waist and pulled them up for him. I pulled the handcuffs from my black tactical vest but struggled to get them on his wrists. He was too big. I pulled my second set of cuffs and looped them in with the first, and then I locked the cuffs behind his back. I quickly checked around his waist to make sure there were no weapons, then patted down the remainder of his body. We rolled him over to a seated position.

"I'm cool, I'm cool."

"Why did you run?"

"Man, I wasn't running. I was just going out to check on some laundry."

"Check on laundry? You started running out the door, and when you saw me, you ran away from me! Didn't you hear me yell to stop and get on the ground?" the local police officer said.

"No sir, I didn't see you."

Hardly believable. The officer was an extremely large man with biceps popping out of his sleeves. We stood Demetrius up and gave him another full search before proceeding to our vehicle and putting him inside. I asked Demetrius if he knew why we arrested him.

"Man, I had that car too long. But y'all shirts say 'Federal Agents' though."

"Right, we're not here for the car; you're under arrest for federal fraud charges."

I showed him the warrant.

"Before I tell you anything further, I will read you your rights."

I read him his Miranda Warnings, you know, the phrases you see on television "you have the right to remain silent, you have the right to an attorney," and all that good stuff.

Demetrius declined to speak to us without an attorney present. I, then, declined to tell him anything further. We transported him to a county facility for the evening.

That night the team went to have a beer. My first arrest. No injuries; that's a "W."

The next day we picked up Demetrius and brought him to a federal detention facility where he would be held until his initial appearance. Demetrius faced several fraud charges including false statements in application for a U.S. passport. The case never went to trial though. Demetrius pled guilty. I was present during his sentencing. He tried to tell the judge that it was all a mistake. The judge wasn't buying it. How can it be a mistake? He pled guilty. The judge sentenced him to sixteen months in a federal prison.

Demetrius was my first experience chasing down and arresting someone, but it certainly was not my last. Houston seemed to be wrought with these types of cases. I've heard from some other DS agents that their respective field offices have no cases or no "action." Too bad for them. Although DS may not be known for our extensive criminal investigative reach, we still had some pretty decent case work in Houston.

The leadership in Houston during this time was outstanding. My new boss Patrick was an excellent leader. As a former Marine, he wanted in on the action. Agent safety was paramount in his mind. He thought in order to mitigate threats to our safety, we had to be aggressive—within the parameters of the law, of course.

Several months later, Dirk and I were asked to help a fellow agent arrest a Nigerian citizen who was wanted on federal fraud charges. He stole the identity of a deceased person and used that stolen information as his own in the application for his U.S. passport. The case agent was a guy named Brett. Brett developed a witness in this case who was willing to help. The witness named Feng was the owner of a passport services business. This service assisted applicants in completing, filing, and ensuring all the criteria for a passport application were met. The Nigerian citizen was one of his clients.

The plan was for Feng to remain in the office in downtown Houston with Dirk and I. At a predetermined time, Feng would call the Nigerian subject to tell him that he was ready to make the passport exchange. The Nigerian subject would then go into a Starbucks, that was previously identified, to meet Feng. In theory, as the subject walked up to the Starbucks, agents would identify him and swoop in to make the arrest. Feng, by being in the office miles away, would be out of harm's way, and by having the Nigerian get out of his car for the exchange, the agents would hopefully avoid a vehicle pursuit.

In this line of work, however, rarely does a plan ever work out exactly as expected. This was no different. As Dirk monitored Feng's phone call to the Nigerian, I was on speaker phone with Brett. Brett could hear Feng's part of the conversation. Feng told the Nigerian that he was waiting inside the Starbucks and that he should come inside. The Nigerian, a career criminal, was conducting surveillance on the place. He didn't see Feng. As DS agents and local police scoured the parking lot looking for a vehicle with the Nigerian in it, the Nigerian was also looking out for the first sign of cops. The Nigerian and Feng must have hung up, called each other back, and argued over the course of four or five phone calls. He was becoming suspicious and was beginning to sense something was amiss. The agents had to make a move.

I convinced Brett to let us come to the Starbucks with Feng. As he pondered the idea and ran it by a supervisor, Dirk and I were already running out of the building to our car. We put Feng in the backseat of the grey Chevrolet Impala, and we raced to the Galleria area of Houston. Driving at a regular speed, getting to the Galleria area from downtown could take 15–20 minutes. Dirk was driving fast. We had the lights and sirens blaring. The vehicle, however, had no "light bars" on top of the car like a traditional police cruiser. This made it very difficult for anyone to see us as we sped down the highway.

Since we weren't easily identifiable as cops, I wanted to help expedite. I thought it was a good idea to hang out the window with my badge in hand, just like in the movies, and encourage people out of the way. I yelled, "Police, move, move, move!" as if we were in a high-speed chase about to crack the crime of the century. It didn't work, but it was fun.

Dirk and I made it to the Galleria in just over ten minutes. Excellent driving from the turtle. We were now within range of radio traffic from the arrest team. I heard someone on the radio say, "That's him. He's in the black car, turning right out of the parking lot. HPD, go ahead and light him up." This was an indication for a Houston police marked cruiser to make a traffic stop on our behalf.

As we heard this on the radio, Dirk and I saw a black car coming in our direction. Then we saw the lights of the Houston police cruiser come on. The car slowed for a second then sped up. He was coming in our direction at a high rate of speed. Dirk turned left into oncoming traffic putting me, on the passenger side, right in front of the speeding Nigerian. "Bro, what the fuck!" I yelled. Dirk laughed. Then, all of a sudden, the car cut left, jumped over the median into the opposite side of the road's oncoming traffic. It quickly turned into a shopping center almost on two wheels.

"Turn around, turn around!" I yelled. Dirk flipped the car around and followed in behind the cruiser and a couple other DS vehicles. As we entered the parking lot, I saw the Nigerian bail from his vehicle and begin to roll. The vehicle kept going across parking spots as it smashed into one, two, three cars. He rolled several times as he hit the ground, and I began telling Dirk to stop. "Stop! Let me out! Let me out!" I screamed. I wanted to catch this dude. I figured, hell, there are two cars already chasing him; somebody had to be on the ground to snatch him. I literally had to start elbowing Dirk so that he would hear me. He was too focused and hardly noticed me yelling for him to stop.

Finally, Dirk let me out. I ran across the parking lot and saw the Nigerian as he approached the back of a building. He went to the right of it, running directly for the cross street ahead of him. The other agents followed in their vehicles. I attempted to predetermine where he would go, thinking he'd turn left once he got to the street. I went to the left side of the building into a back alleyway in the hopes that he'd hit the sidewalk, and I'd cut him off if he turned left. As I ran to the alleyway, I hurdled a row of bushes that must have been six feet, maybe even ten feet tall. Or, at least, that's what I tell people. They were only maybe a foot high. Whatever, I was in the moment.

As I jumped over the large set of bushes, I remember my mind slowing and thinking, "I wonder if any chicks are watching this." Then my feet hit the ground. I looked left and right, no chicks. Damnit. I sprinted through the alleyway and saw a guy across the street pointing and yelling, "That way! That way!" I turned right, ran down the sidewalk to the front corner of the building, and then right again back into the parking lot as I saw the the Nigerian on the ground. One of the agents kneeled on his back to cuff him. I ran up, feeling like I was last in the race. I kneeled next to him and said "you can't run from the feds." I thought I was cool, like in the movies cool, hooking up a criminal on a one-count passport charge. Whatever. Mission accomplished.

That night several of us went out for a beer and told our story to anyone who would listen. Dirk and I tell a pretty good story together. Dirk's wife was the first to hear it. As we excitedly replayed the day's events, she didn't believe us. It just so happened it was April 1st: April Fools Day. It took several other agents to arrive and confirm that this chase, no shit, happened for her to believe us.

My two-year tour in Houston was a lot of fun. I had an outstanding group of agents, excellent leadership, significant autonomy, and some pretty good casework for DS standards. I was constantly busy helping other agencies with cases or assisting in arrests. The experiences I had in Houston with investigations would give me a solid foundation to investigate further cases when working overseas. The largest case of my career, however, was in process. I was to lead one of the most robust arrest operations in the HFO's history, and it was only a few months away until execution.

Chapter 2

OPERATION WRECKED SAFARI

In October of 2009, the Director of the Diplomatic Security Service was visiting Houston on his national tour. Agents in the office were scheduled to have a lunch with him before his departure. On that day, as agents were leaving to go to a lunch, I was asked to stay back and assist with a phone call. The call was from a passport services clerk at the U.S. Passport Agency, just down on the lower floors of the building from the DS Houston Field Office. The clerk told me that a girl who arrived to pick up her passport was acting suspicious. The girl's passport application had multiple indicators of fraud, including misspellings, and missing information. The Texas identification card she was using to pick up the passport also appeared to be tampered with. They asked if I could interview her as soon as possible. I got her biographical data (name, date of birth, and social security number) and told the clerk we'd be in touch.

One of my agent colleagues, Nikki, helped me out on the case. We began to build a file with a copy of the passport application, criminal records, and other information from our databases that helped us build a profile in advance of encountering her. After we had a good grasp of who this individual was, we made our way down to the passport office to talk to her.

As Nikki and I took the elevator down to the passport agency, we discussed our game plan. I would step out of the elevator first, button hook right, and Nikki would go left. I'd then proceed to the door and kick through it. Nikki would commence a tactical roll into the room where she'd hop to her feet, pull out her gun, and we'd take the subject into custody. Easy day.

Just kidding. We don't do that stuff. We walked up and asked her name, then asked her if she would come with us. Simple as that. She had a friend, and the friend wanted to come too. The girls' names were Tyra and Denae.

Both Tyra and Denae were of African-American descent. They were approximately eighteen years old, born and raised in South Houston, and both high school dropouts. Their clothes appeared dirty; their hair disheveled. When I spoke to them, they were both polite. But I could also hear the nervousness in their voices.

As we rode up the elevator to our office, I asked a few basic questions to the primary suspect: Tyra.

"Tyra, where are you traveling to?"

"Africa."

"Oh yeah? Where in Africa?"

"I don't know, just Africa."

"OK. Africa is a large continent; you don't know where you're going in Africa?"

"No."

I thought that was interesting. So then I said, "What are you going do in Africa?"

"I'm gonna go see the animals."

"OK. What animals are your favorite?"

"Uhh, I like 'em all."

I laughed, probably out loud, as I thought that was a great answer. "What do you do for work?"

"Ah, I don't work."

"Really, so how will you pay for the trip?"

"My uncle is gonna pay for it."

"OK. What does your uncle do?"

"I don't know."

"You don't know what your uncle does for work?"

"Nope."

Within the time the elevator made it from the 4th floor to the 23rd floor, we determined that something was definitely awry. Tyra couldn't answer basic questions, never looked me in the eye, and appeared nervous. We walked into the office, and I sat the girls in different rooms. They were not under arrest, so we made sure they knew that they could go to the restroom and offered them some water and snacks. The law states that if an agent has "reasonable suspicion" that criminal activity is afoot, then an agent can detain an individual for a reasonable amount of time. So we did. We had questions to ask.

The room the girls were in had no windows and only one door. There was nothing on the walls; it was just bare white sheetrock. There was a long table in the middle with two chairs on one side of the table and only one on the other. Miranda Warnings and other printed documents were placed on the table.

I notified our supervisors that we detained two suspects and that we needed support. A couple of the agents came back early from lunch to help. We discussed our game plan and went at it. I went in one room with a colleague, and two other agents went in the other. We interviewed the girls separately so that they could not copy each other's stories. As we began to ask questions, we informed Tyra and Denae of their rights, made sure they knew this was a voluntary interview, they were not under arrest, and that they were free to leave at anytime.

As the interview progressed, I learned that these girls were not intending to travel for enjoyment, to see animals, or anything of that nature. They didn't have jobs, no money to travel, had never been overseas, and didn't know who they were going to stay with in "Africa."

After about thirty minutes, I left the room and discussed our findings with my colleagues. We all agreed; something nefarious was going on, and the girls weren't telling the truth. During our discussions, an agent came in and told me that while I was interviewing the girls, the security guard from downstairs called the office. He stated that the individual who had escorted the suspects into the passport agency "bolted" as we took them up the elevator. I asked the security guard to pull up the camera footage so we could review it.

By this time the supervisors had returned from lunch. I went to brief one of the them with what I learned so far. We discussed options and a strategy to extract more information. We decided on a ruse. We'd tell the girls that the dude they came to the passport agency with was an accused drug trafficker, and we took him into custody. We'd also tell them that he said they were "drug mules"; someone used to traffick drugs. Lastly, we'd tell the girls that the he was being taken down to the Drug Enforcement Administration (DEA) for processing.

I decided that we'd try the ruse on one girl at a time to see how they would react and if we could play them off of one another. I interviewed Tyra first.

"Tyra, I'm afraid we have some bad news. That dude you came with, he's under arrest." "What dude? I didn't come with no dude."

"Tyra, we know you did; we have it on video. He also implicated you in more severe crimes than we expected."

"What you mean?"

"Well, he's a known drug trafficker, and he says y'all are drug mules."

"Huh, mules? What's that? I don't know no dude."

"That means you carry and deliver drugs to people on his behalf, specifically cocaine."

"What?! Nah, Ah, no way!"

"Well, that's what he told us. Unless you have another story?"

"Man, fuck that dude. All he told me was that I need to go to Africa, get married to his cousin, and come back. That's it. I don't know nothin' about no drugs."

"So, he wanted you to go to Africa to marry someone?"

"Yeah."

"Who?"

"I don't even know his name. I just was supposed to go there. They pick me up at the airport, we go eat or something, get married, take some pictures, and I sign some papers. That's it."

I took this information and discussed it with my colleagues. One of them mentioned the possibility of human trafficking or smuggling, and this was a tactic he'd heard of before. Individuals would use the "Fiancé Visa" to marry Americans and come live in the U.S. but was that all that was going on here? We weren't sure, so I went back in. This time I would talk to Denae.

I used the same ruse; except, this time, I wasted no time getting to the point.

"Denae, the dude you were downstairs with, he's been arrested. He's going to be booked by the DEA then sent to the Federal Correction Center. He said you are a drug mule."

"What dude?"

"The one you came here with."

"I came here with Tyra, that's it."

"Ok well, we have video footage that you came with a male, and he said you are a drug mule."

"What's that?"

So I explained it all over again.

"I ain't no drug mule."

"OK great. Then you wanna tell me what's going on here?"

By this time we had pulled Denae's passport application and criminal history report. She was a co-conspirator, so we needed as much information as we could get. Denae was much harder though.

"Ain't nothin goin on. I'm just trying to go to Africa too," she said.

So then we told her that Tyra confessed. Still, Denae was tough; she wasn't going to budge. So rather than waste our time with an uncooperative suspect, we paused, regrouped, and went back to Tyra.

"Tyra, that guy you came here with, what was his name?"

"I think his name was Alex or something."

"OK, how did you meet him?"

"Through Denae."

"Well, Denae says she doesn't know him."

"Well, she's lying."

"OK, and how did you get here today?"

"He brought us in his white truck. It's like a work truck or something."

"A work truck?"

"Yeah, like the kind you use to carry cars."

"You mean a tow truck?"

"Yeah, like that."

"Can you describe him for me?"

"Yeah, he African."

"African American?"

"No, like African. But he's a light-colored African. And he has an accent too."

"About how tall?"

"Maybe this much taller than me." She stood up and put her hand over her head.

So I estimated: 5'10" or so. She also told me she thought he looked as if he weighed around 200 pounds. None of that needed to be exact; we just wanted to start to build a picture.

By this point other agents were already downstairs pulling video footage. The camera tracked the guy as he left the passport office and went to his truck. Lucky for us, he was parked directly across the street from the federal building. We identified him on his departure from the building as he got into a white tow truck. Even better, we could see the business label on the side of his truck and the full license plate.

So now we had a description of the individual, description of the vehicle, and camera footage of both. We had license plate numbers and a business name on the side of the truck. If you're not familiar with investigations, this was plenty to start with.

I asked our investigative analyst to run the plates. The plates came back as an exact match for a white wrecker truck. Alex Moloko, his date of birth, height 5' 10", weight 190, social security number, and his place of birth: Kenya. Well, that explains the accent and where in Africa. Too bad for the girls; Kenya has excellent animal "watching."

We used all of that information to build a robust profile on Moloko. How did he get to the U.S.? How long has he been here for? Who are his next of kin and acquaintances? What are his addresses? What about this business? We ran with those questions and began to investigate and develop the case more extensively. We contacted Immigrations and Customs Enforcement (ICE) to check his immigrations status, Customs and Border Protection (CBP) to get the specifics on his crossings, and the State of Texas to provide detailed data from his driver license application and more.

This all happened within the hour. I wanted more information from the girls, but I knew this was all I'd get out of them, and the time with which I could continue to detain them was ending. I needed to allow them to leave. I told the girls that I'd be by their homes to discuss this further in the coming weeks. I advised them that it was best not to associate with Alex anymore, but if he does ask, I recommend not telling him about our interview. Before they left, we confirmed their address matched with what was in our databases. For now, we were set.

Over the next several months, I continued to build the case and discovered a web of individuals facilitating the smuggling of Kenyan nationals into the country by two means: through educational institutions or by sham marriages. Within a couple of weeks, I had enough information, so I went to present this case to the U.S. Attorney's Office. The case was named "Operation Wrecked Safari." You know, wrecker truck, seeing animals in Africa, we "wrecked" their trip. C'mon, you get it. I thought it fit.

After a few weeks, I arrived at the U.S. Attorney's office to present my case. I went through my notes as I prepared to pitch the case to the assigned Assistant U.S. Attorney, Kebharu. I had pictures and boxes of documents laid out all over the table. I had only been an agent for about six months at this point, and my administrative skills could have used some fine tuning. But Kebharu took it in stride. He and I worked well together and our personalities clicked, so it made life easier. Although, every time I brought information about the case to him, he'd jokingly complain, "Damn Cody, you brought me this fraud case with all these intricate details and documents!" We always had a laugh as I continued to bombard him with emails and documents. Fraud cases are tedious.

For the next ten months, I filled my time with database checks, multiple interviews, surveillance, subpoenas, warrants, undercover work, and report writing. Lots of report writing. In those ten months, we revealed a large web of Kenyan nationals smuggling other Kenyan nationals into the country by facilitating visa issuance through fraudulent education aspirations or marriages. It was so large we had to cut off our investigation into more suspects. We just didn't have the manpower to handle a case that continued to grow.

The Kenyans used three primary tactics to perpetrate this fraud. The first scheme was the misuse of student visas. The Kenyans would present fictitious information on their visa application about their intent to study at a college in the United States. They'd also provide fraudulent Kenyan educational documents, easy to get in Kenya. In this particular case, they applied to Texas Southern University in Houston. Many of these Kenyans had previously applied for other types of visas to travel and visit the United States. But most of them had been denied because they didn't meet the stringent visa requirements. The student visa, however, was an easier visa to manipulate. If their application was approved, they would come to America and, once here, generally only attend one or two semesters. Some of the Kenyans didn't even attend university as they realized they weren't held accountable by anyone.

The second scheme was just as simple. The Kenyans would find a willing American citizen female partner, pay her some money, buy her clothes and shoes, then put her on a plane to Kenya where they would meet with the Kenyan family members at the airport. They would get married in Kenya, take some photos, sign some documents, and there you have it. The American would then attend an interview with their new Kenyan "spouse" at the nearest U.S. Embassy or Consulate where they would apply for a fiancé visa. Granted, it didn't always work. The State Department Consular Officers who issued fiancé visas often asked the right questions, discovered the fraud, then denied the visa. But that didn't deter anyone from trying. There is little or no penalty in Kenya for trying this and getting caught.

The third scheme was very similar and a combination of the two. For those Kenyans who already made it to the U.S., they would just find a willing U.S. citizen female participant in Houston, pay them money, get married at the courthouse, and then five years later, apply for U.S. citizenship.

This type of criminal activity happens frequently. It is prevalent in just about every major city in the United States. The U.S. government does not have the manpower, time, or money to investigate all of these people involved in the massive amount of immigration fraud schemes. Furthermore, those agencies that that do investigate these schemes have cases that are often turned down by U.S. attorneys offices because of the weak sentencing guidelines for perpetrators of these types of crimes. It's shameful, but it's reality.

As the months passed, this case was my main focus. I narrowed the case down to five primary targets and investigated them thoroughly. I also turned my sights on Denae. I learned she was more heavily involved than Tyra. I made many trips to Denae's home and interviewed her mother, her sister, and other family members several times over. It turns out it was a family affair. The mother was the first person of the family to carry out this fraud with the Kenyans. Once the daughters got wind of her "success" and the money she was receiving, they wanted to be involved as well. Three of the daughters, some cousins, and friends of the family were all colluding to defraud the government.

This family, however, was not my main target. Although they were also guilty as co-conspirators of the fraud, Kebharu and I knew that we needed someone to be a witness. Our argument was that these women from poor neighborhoods of South

Houston were taken advantage of and preyed on. We enlisted their cooperation in exchange for not prosecuting them.

After almost of a year of investigating, it was time to execute our plan for arrest. One morning in late 2010, I was with my team outside a CVS store at 0515. DS Agents, Harris County Sheriff's Officers, and Immigrations and Customs Enforcement Officers were all part of the team. The day prior I had received a federal warrant for the arrest of Alex Moloko and four other associates. I briefed a plan to make entry on Moloko's home. At that same time, DS agents were briefing three other teams in different locations in a five-square-mile radius to arrest the other suspects. The plan was to conduct a simultaneous "hit" on homes in an attempt to arrest Moloko and the others: five warrants for suspects at four different locations.

Once the brief was completed, we proceeded to Moloko's house. It was still dark outside. Four vehicles sat parked strategically around the perimeter of the two-story home watching to see if there was any movement inside. It was too early; this guy was a lazy criminal. He wasn't up yet. As 0600 arrived, we approached the home. Six of us on the "stack," or entry team, that was going to enter the home. The remainder of agents and officers would stay on the perimeter. We were all kitted up in our black tactical vests that read "POLICE" on the front and "Federal Agent" on the back. Most of us were in jeans, t-shirts, and sneakers. Our perimeter agents began to take their assigned positions, and they called in over the radio, "Alpha, set," "Bravo, set," and so on, distinguishing what side of the house they were located.

After receiving confirmation from all perimeter agents, I gave the signal to execute. The agent commenced with three big knocks: boom, Boom, BOOM.

"Police, with a warrant, open the door!" Then again, "Police, with a warrant, open the door!"

This went on for about 30 seconds or so. Thirty long seconds. For those of you who are not familiar with the law, police cannot just kick in a door and come in your home even if we do have a warrant. We have to announce three things: (1) who we are (Police), (2) why we are here (we have a warrant), and (3) instructions (open the door). Then we must wait a reasonable amount of time for the subject to get to the door based on a number of factors: size of the house, time of day, etc. Just enough time for them to get a weapon and come to the door; awesome.

I pounded on the door for what felt like an eternity then finally called out "breacher up." The breacher brought up the "ram" and was about to smash the door when I heard someone on the other side. We kept yelling, "Open the door! Open the door!" Finally the door slowly opened; it was Moloko. The team rushed in. The first man shoved Moloko back and to the ground as the second and third went left and right. The remainder of the six-person team followed, pushing deeper in the home. We filled the bottom floor of the house, checking anywhere a person could hide.

One agent noticed a stairwell and called it out, "Stairwell left!" then "I got movement!" when he noticed a small wobbly figure come around the corner. It was a toddler; she was at the top of the stairs. She wasn't crying. Just curious as she made her way down to us, feet first and on her belly. One of the ladies on our team immediately stepped up and tended to the toddler, taking her off the stairs. The remainder of the guys went up to clear the upper bedrooms.

"Upstairs, clear," I heard.

Roger that. I radioed out to the guys on the perimeter, "All clear, all clear, all clear."

We handcuffed Moloko and sat him in a chair. I asked if he knew why we were there which, of course, he denied. He was the facilitator of this massive fraud scheme. He knew what was up, but he wasn't going to talk to us. I allowed him to call someone to come and take care of the baby. His wife soon arrived and was briefly interviewed as a co-conspirator. We decided to leave her so that she could take care of the toddler.

On our way to the office, I called the other teams to check the status of their arrest operations. They informed me that they were successful in arresting three of the remaining four suspects. Robert, who lived with his brother Alonso (who was also a suspect), was not at his home at the time of the arrest warrant execution. We'd have to track him down and arrest him at a later time.

As I arrived back to the office, it was abuzz. Agents were processing and interviewing. I went in to each interview in an attempt to ask a few questions, but they all lawyered up. Fine by me. We had all the information we needed.

Shortly after arriving, I received a call from a team of agents looking for our final subject: Robert. "Cody, we need y'all to get here quickly. We have a marked HPD unit out here but only two agents," the agent said. I grabbed three of our best agents and made our way over to the location.

The drive took us about fifteen minutes. Upon arrival the agents on the ground briefed up as the uniformed local police officer watched the door. The plan was set, and the team moved toward the door of the second story apartment building. We slowly creeped up the steps. Here we go again, boom, Boom, BOOM, "Police, with a warrant, open the door," one of the guys pounded. Within seconds the door opened; the girl that opened the door was put to the ground instantly. Agents filled in the room, right and left.

"Where is Robert?" I shouted.

"I don't know!"

"Two more rooms in the back; move on them."

The rooms in the back of the house were directly across from each other. One agent keyed in and held his position at the door on the left. Another agent and I paused for a second at the door on the right, then I nodded my head and we went for it. "Get on the ground, get on the ground!" we yelled upon entry as we aimed our pistols at the individual in the room. A male wearing a hoodie and a knit cap immediately dropped to the floor. I walked up to him, removed the knit cap from his head, and asked, "what's your name?!" He told me. It wasn't Robert.

"Where is Robert?"

"I don't know; he was here earlier."

"Fuck it, next room. Stay here and watch this dude," I told the agent.

The next room had two agents already stacked on it. Same thing as we made entry.

"Get on the ground, get on the ground!" The man who was laying on the bed quickly rolled off onto his stomach. I pushed past the other agents and jumped on him, put my knee in his back, and asked, "are you Robert?" I looked at his face as he confirmed.

"You're under arrest for...wait, did you just shit yourself?"

"I'm sorry, sir. I'm really scared. I think I just farted."

I chuckled a bit. We rolled Robert over in handcuffs and searched him. He smelled awful.

"Bro, no need to be scared. We won't hurt you. But, seriously. Are you sure you didn't shit yourself? We can let you go to the bathroom if you need it."

"No, sir. I don't think so. My stomach is just very nervous."

"OK, cool, but listen. If you need the bathroom, please let us know. We don't need any accidents in the car."

"Yes, sir."

We packed up Robert and made our way back to the office. I remember on the car ride home Robert randomly commenting on how nice we were.

"You are very nice, sir. Thank you," Robert said in a strong Kenyan accent.

"Robert, we just came into the house and arrested you. Why are you thanking us?"

"Sir, in my country, I would be bleeding and have broken bones. So thank you. Americans are very nice."

I wasn't sure if he was trying to flatter us thinking he could wiggle his way out of his predicament or if he was being genuine. Regardless, he was in good spirits for just being arrested. We all shared a good laugh as we chatted the whole way back to the office.

Fast forward three years later to 2013. I was back in Houston to testify at this trial. I had left Houston in December of 2010 for Baghdad. The case had been pushed off for so many years for a number of reasons, but now all of the subjects were going to trial. I flew back from what was my current assignment in Ho Chi Minh City, Vietnam, to testify.

It was great to be back in Houston. I was ecstatic to see some of the other agents that helped with the case. I was also pumped to see Kebharu. He and I had become good friends over the years and kept in touch. This was going to be fun.

We met with Kebharu days before the trial to help make sure every detail was accurate. A fraud case of this magnitude has some serious minutiae and often times copious amount of documents to review. Kebharu was all in at this point though. He knew the case backwards and forwards. We prepped for a few days and would soon go to trial.

I remember each time it was the prosecution's turn to speak. Kebharu stood in that courtroom and killed it. His charisma, intellect, and swag were relentless. No form of evidence could be presented by the defense that he couldn't counter to put them back in check. It was impressive.

The trial proceeded as planned. Witnesses took the stand, and the jury heard arguments from both sides. Then it was my time to testify. Kebharu asked me a couple basic questions about my background, my duties, and my responsibilities as a DS agent in Houston. Then he got into the case. Together we knocked it out of the park, in my humble opinion.

What I recall the most was the cross-examination by one of the defense attorneys. I remember this attorney sweating profusely shortly before he had to present his case. He was overly nice outside the courtroom when I'd encounter him during breaks, but when he examined me, he went off.

"Agent Perron, how long were you in my client's house?"

"Approximately 20–30 minutes, sir."

"20–30 minutes? What were you searching for?"

"We weren't searching for anything."

"OK, so you were in the house for 20–30 minutes, without a search warrant, and you say you weren't searching. Then what took so long?"

"Well, sir, there was a baby in the house. We allowed Mr. Moloko to call someone to come take care of the baby. We made sure he was able to get dressed and get some cash in case he needed some while in the federal correction center. Then his wife arrived, so we let them chat a bit."

I'm pretty sure he didn't expect that answer. He was trying to build a case to the jury that we infringed on his client's rights by being there and "searching" for something when, in fact, we were doing all we could to make sure Moloko's child was taken care of.

Still he went on, "Agent Perron, why couldn't you find Angela Whitmore?" he asked. Angela was the first wife of Moloko. I searched for her frequently in multiple neighborhoods in Houston and had no luck. Residents didn't necessarily want to talk to police. We knew she was into prostitution, crack smoking, and maybe even dealing. She was impossible to find and really not so relevant to the case. But this dude thought she was, so I responded.

"Sir, we searched for her for almost a year. Residents were uncooperative, and she is heavily embedded inside her neighborhood in South Houston."

"So you couldn't find her?" He shook his head, put his hand on his chin, and paused. "The U.S. government can find Osama Bin Laden in Pakistan, but you can't find Angela Whitmore?"

"Mutha fucker, I work in a cubicle!"...is what I wanted to say. Instead, I said, "No, sir."

The jury wasn't buying it. He finished his line of questioning, and I came out of there unscathed.

This same attorney, one of four attorneys representing these defendants, blew it on his final argument. He proceeded to pound his fist and yelled, "We know how it feels to see lights and hear sirens with guns pointed at our face when Police come to our house!!!" He lamented to an all white jury of grandfathers and grandmothers. What the fuck was he thinking?

The trial ended, and we came out on top. The four defendants that chose to proceed to trial were all found guilty of visa fraud, marriage fraud, and conspiracy to commit marriage fraud. Two of the defendants were also convicted of unlawful procurement of citizenship or naturalization. As a result of the unlawful procurement of citizenship, the court revoked the fraudulently acquired U.S. citizenship of Moloko and one other defendant. They were each sentenced to sixteen months' imprisonment. Robert and another defendant were sentenced to six months' imprisonment. The fifth defendant, who opted out of trial, pleaded guilty to conspiracy to commit marriage fraud and tampering with a witness. He was sentenced to 21 months' imprisonment.[2]

Operation Wrecked Safari was the highlight of my investigations career in DS. Although the penalties for these crimes aren't the most severe, we brought to light issues that needed to be addressed and prosecuted. That's a victory for the HFO and Southern District of Texas U.S. Attorney's Office.

---

2 S. Elmilady and K. Smith, "Prosecuting Marriage Fraud Conspiracies. Lifting the Veil of Sham Marriages," *Border Issues* 62, no. 6 (November 2014): 47.

Chapter 3

BOMBS OVER BIDEN

In June of 2010, I was in the back of a C-130 Hercules military transport aircraft on my way to the Baghdad International Airport (BIAP). As we descended to the tarmac, the aircraft began circling as it lowered in altitude. It was a common practice to execute these evasive maneuvers in an attempt to avoid enemy fire. I sat in a webbed seat with the seat belt hanging off the side. I was wearing a flak jacket and had my helmet on my lap. The aircraft was loud and crammed, and the ride was bumpy, but I didn't care. I was excited to be in Iraq.

Upon landing, the aircraft taxied to the "American side" of the BIAP. On this side was Camp Victory, a U.S. military base. On the base was a small U.S. State Department facility deemed "Sully Compound," named after Stephen Sullivan—a DS Special Agent who was killed in a terrorist attack on a motorcade in Mosul in 2005. This is where I'd be waiting until they unloaded my suitcase and gave me a lift to the U.S. Embassy, also known as the New Embassy Compound (NEC).

I was dazed and confused at this point. I had traveled all the way from Houston, was picked up at the international airport in

Kuwait, and taken to a hotel where I wasn't allowed to purchase a beer. Then, early the next morning, I was picked up and taken to the Ali Al Salem U.S. Air Force base to catch my deluxe flight to Baghdad. I was ready to be at the embassy already.

After about an hour of waiting, I boarded the "Rhino" bus, and we began our journey. The Rhino is a specially made steel bus that could allegedly protect us from enemy munitions. Fortunately, it wasn't tested on my ride down the infamous "Route Irish" on our way to the NEC. Just outside the bus, in front, back, and on the side was our protective motorcade in armored Suburbans. The motorcade was led by one DS agent in charge and an experienced Triple Canopy, or TC, contractor as shift leader. The contractors from TC encompassed the majority of protection details. All of the contractors were very experienced. Many were former Blackwater, and all were either military veterans or experienced law enforcement professionals prior to coming to TC.

After a fairly expeditious and non-eventful trip down Route Irish, we entered the Baghdad "Green Zone." The Green Zone is a "secure area" inside central Baghdad that houses several foreign embassies and multiple Iraqi Government Ministries and offices. Although the area is more secure than the remainder of Baghdad, it certainly had security vulnerabilities and was a frequent target of terrorist attacks.

Inside the Green Zone was the massive U.S. Embassy complex. Some described it as a university. Sure, that's it. A university surrounded by T-walls and concertina wire, with armed guards patrolling, concrete bunkers every couple hundred yards, and about a 10:1 male to female ratio.

On the other hand, I could see how it would be mistaken for a university. There were the debaucherous Thursday nights at the infamous Baghdaddy's bar where the pours were heavy, the price was right, and the bromances flourished. Plenty of barbecue pits were spread about the compound to gather with friends. There was a soccer field, a grassy knoll, two full gyms, indoor and outdoor swimming pools, and a half-court indoor basketball court. The dining facility was pretty damn good also. One night a week was lobster and steak night. And on Sundays the dessert cart literally chased me up and down the aisles of the chow hall until I took a slice of the fucking cheesecake.

The Staff Diplomatic Apartments, or SDAs, were another benefit. Most were two bedroom apartments inside 3–4 story concrete structures. The tenants of each apartment would share a common bathroom and kitchen; but, all in all, it was pretty legit. Unfortunately, the TC contractors didn't fare as well, but they had their own little paradise deemed "Man Camp." I remember walking into that place in my first week to meet some of the guys when I heard gangster rap music blaring from afar. As we approached, I saw jacked, tattooed, shirtless dudes eating full steaks with their hands and cooking beans in the same can it was packaged in. Savages. It was awesome.

My favorite part of the embassy was the "grab and go." It was pretty much the 7/11 of the embassy compound. There were several 24/7 grab and gos where anyone could walk in, grab a coffee, soft drink, sandwich, cookie, small bowls of cereal, and, if you're lucky, a Rip-It energy drink. Or, if you're a special kind of guy, as many Rip-Its as your shredded biceps can hold.

I came to Baghdad to be one of the Agents In Charge (AIC) of protection details. Each protection detail and motorcade had one direct hire special agent acting as the AIC. The remainder of the detail, as previously mentioned, was made up of TC contractors. The vehicles used in each motorcade were armored Chevrolet Suburbans sometimes accompanied by "little bird" helicopters doing reconnaissance along our routes.

The AIC's responsibility is the overall command of the motorcade and the close protection of the "principal" or "protectee," the person being protected. The operational and tactical command fell to the shift leader. The shift leader is the continuity and tactical specialist of the detail. Most shift leaders are senior to their teammates by their "time in service" in the area of operations with TC or Blackwater and take responsibility for the planning and execution of the "Missions." The tactical commander is third in charge and the navigator. He plans all routes: primary, secondary, and tertiary. And, during the mission, he sits in the first vehicle, effectively getting the protection detail to our location. All the other contractors are considered shooters or drivers, and one trained medic is part of every detail. Each detail also has a Personal Protective Specialist (PPS) who is a local Iraqi that works for the U.S. Government. He carried a gun but was mostly utilized as an interpreter. At one point, Iraqi National Police or INPs were embedded in our motorcades, but the TC guys didn't trust them, so we often went without those guys.

So what are the the missions? Anytime a diplomat needed to go outside the Green Zone, thus into the "Red Zone," they were taken by a protection detail. Where did they go? You name it. Iraqi ministries that fell outside of the Green Zone, refugee camps, U.S. or Iraqi military installations, and more. Most of the time the diplomats were limited to "business" dealings, but oftentimes their business was articulated as a dinner at a nice restaurant to have a couple of drinks with their contacts.

The office I worked in was called the "POD." The Protective Operations Division (POD) was located in a large office with no internal walls, kind of like a squad bay with carpets. Each AIC had a small cubicle connected to another cubicle where we'd check Facebook and watch YouTube. I mean, where we planned missions and executed professional correspondence. The POD was the place to be. We generally had a great group of dudes. The contractors were often in there, and the shit talk was perpetual.

The POD was made up of two different elements: Independent Protection Details (IDP) and the Ambassadors Protection Detail (APD). The IPD teams were divided into three different units. Each unit had approximately seven high-profile protection teams and two low-profile teams. IDP teams took out your regular diplomats for their business dealings. The high-profile teams conducted operations with multiple armored Suburbans for a team that moved with protectees and three or four with teams that went to the venues in advance, without a protectee, to set up security. Oftentimes a pair of little-bird helicopters accompanied the teams or conducted a reconnaissance to give us the best intelligence on our routes.

The low-profile teams used more covert style tactics to move around the red zone. The guys on low-pro were recruited specifically by the shift leader and others on the team. Because of their unique operation, they needed to be able to trust the others on the team. These groups of dudes were as solid as can be. You can't miss the low-pro guys: plaid button downs, skinny slacks, and chucks. They also had great hair. The best hair.

On second thought, scratch that. The Ambassadors Protection Detail (APD) had the best hair. APD was the team that took out the Ambassador and the Deputy Chief of Mission to their meetings in both the green and red zone. These guys were also highly recruited and highly capable. But, to be in APD, you'd have to enjoy wearing a suit and be on call for random "pop up" movements at a moment's notice. The APD guys didn't share a the physical office space with us peasants in the POD building. They had their own cubicles in the main chancery office building. Many of us in IPD, however, didn't care to wear suits in 100° weather. We liked wearing our 5.11 pants, untucked shirts, and hats.

The daily activities of the POD agents were to attend an intelligence briefing every morning, brief with the team, go out on a mission, eat, workout, plan the next day's mission, eat again, maybe workout again or have a drink or two, then sleep. Repeat almost every day for 60 days or the length of each individual's tour. On Thursday nights, however, Baghdaddys came calling, and it was a requirement to engage in intellectual conversation or copious amounts of tomfoolery, usually the latter.

Towards the end of this Baghdad assignment, Vice President (VP) Joe Biden made a trip to Baghdad. The VP was coming to Baghdad to meet with Iraqi and U.S. government officials on the ground. A VP trip, for reference, is an enormous undertaking for security teams particularly in a volatile environment like Iraq.

The U.S. Secret Service team was on the ground weeks in advance planning every movement of the VP from his arrival until his departure. Every move was choreographed. Fortunately for me, I wasn't involved in the tedious planning phases. But I was one of the AICs in the motorcade in the vehicle behind the "press bus." The press travels everywhere with the VP and President. There were so much press and staff that they needed their own bus.

The VP's helicopter set down in a Landing Zone (LZ) near the Embassy and inside the Green Zone. Risking taking him down Route Irish was a "no-go"; and, well, the VP certainly wouldn't ride in a Rhino bus. Nor would a 40-plus vehicle motorcade be too inconspicuous down Route Irish. As the bird landed, tactical helicopters with armed special operations soldiers circled above. The dust was blowing, and the little hair the VP had on his head was waving in the air. I had to turn around as not to be slapped in the face by the debris that the helicopter rotors kicked up. VP Biden was met by the Ambassador. They shook hands, loaded up the motorcade, and made their way to the embassy. The movement went off without incident.

Later that evening, the VP was scheduled to remain on the embassy compound and attend an event at the ambassador's residence. The guests of the event were made up of American and Iraqi officials, some of local provinces. The Iraqi officials were all screened by security before entering the compound.

The Secret Service moved VP Biden from his apartment to the ambassador's residence, approximately 100 yards, by armored Suburban. This was strategic and a good idea since directly across the embassy compound was an apartment complex that was known to have some shady characters living in it. The DS agents working with the Secret Service advised them to utilize the ECMs, or electronic countermeasures, on the vehicles. These ECMs emit a powerful signal so strong that it renders cell phones useless within a certain radius. VP Biden arrived to the ambassador's residence without issue.

On that same evening, I attended a party at the Marine house. The Marine Security Guards who work at the embassy protect the internal infrastructure of the chancery building and other buildings that hold classified material. They are responsible for the physical protection of the U.S. Embassy. The Marine house at most embassies is pretty awesome. This one was no different. It had a pool table, big screen television, and its own bar. On the outside was a basketball court and a sand volleyball pit. They had some tiki torches lit for this party.

I walked over to the party with my friend Jeremy, a Special Agent from the Drug Enforcement Administration (DEA) and former Marine. Jeremy and I stayed at the Marine House for a couple of hours, drinking a couple of beers and eating hot dogs. Most visitors to the Marine House were congregated outside, standing on the basketball court or sitting around a fire. It was a nice night to be out, even for Baghdad standards.

After a couple of hours, Jeremy and I decided to leave the party and make our way back to our respective apartments. As we reached the apartment where VP Biden was staying, we noticed that his motorcade was moving towards us and Secret Service agents were standing outside. Jeremy wanted to stay and watch so he could see the VP up close. I identified myself to the Secret Service agents, some of which remembered me from earlier in the day. They were cool with us standing there so we could get a close up view.

When the VP arrived at his apartment, he remained in the vehicle while he talked on his phone. At this point, I could only assume the Secret Service agents turned off the ECMs so that he could make his call. After a few minutes on the phone, the VP slowly stepped out of the vehicle when, all of a sudden, a loud *swoosh* sound was heard over our heads. I knew what was happening. "Get him inside, get him inside!" I yelled. The Secret Service Agents didn't know what the hell was going on until, right around the time I opened my mouth, a loud blast shook us: *boom!* Then another *swoosh* and *boom* again not too far away from us. They grabbed the VP and rushed him inside the building.

As soon as we heard the first boom, Jeremy said, "Cody, that's at the Marine House!"

"Fuck, let's go!" I said.

We sprinted as fast as we could to the Marine house as we heard more blasts in the distance and around us: *boom, boom.*

"Bro, if that hit on the fucking basketball court, we're looking at mass casualties," I said as we ran.

I got on the radio and called to the Tactical Operations Center (TOC), "We got incoming. Impact near the Marine House."

By this time the C-RAM (Counter Rocket, Artillery, Mortar) horn was sounding across the compound with an intermittent message "Incoming, Incoming, Incoming." The alarm usually sounds before the impact of the mortar when the radar picks up the incoming rocket. But this time, the mortar rounds were shot so low that the radar didn't detect them. This is also why we heard the swoosh so distinctly.

Jeremy and I finally reached the outside of the Marine House and looked inside the gate. No one was outside anymore. Fortunately, no one was on the ground and no blood either. I looked behind me and saw one impact site and the damage it did to the concrete wall.

Then Jeremy said, "Oh shit, Cody. You're standing in the impact site!"

"What the fuck!" I said as I jumped out of it.

We both laughed. That was the second impact site not far from the first.

"Don't worry, bro. It doesn't land in the same place twice!"

"Yeah, clearly! We should probably find some cover."

Jeremy and I went into a nearby concrete bunker, but after about thirty seconds, we soon realized the bunker was lacking key necessities.

"Bro, we don't have beer. We need some beer," I said to Jeremy.

"Hell yeah we do," he agreed.

"Fuck it. Let's make a run for it."

The C-RAM was still blasting as we ran and entered the front door of the Marine House. Once we opened the door, we noticed everyone inside was OK, although several of them were in tears. In a celebration of life, we decided to crack open a beer and have a "we're all still alive party."

"Heeeyyyyy, we're still alive!" someone yelled, as the music started playing. That was one cold and refreshing beer.

After our celebratory libation, Jeremy and I left again, laughing along the way with adrenaline still pumping. We retraced our steps and walked where the mortar hit the ground. It was a pretty sizeable hole, but the spray of the rocks against the nearby wall showed how destructive one of the Iranian-supplied Katyusha rockets can be. If that rocket landed only twenty feet to the right, this would have certainly been a mass casualty event. We were lucky.

On our trip back to our apartments, we saw one of the Secret Service agents. I walked up to him.

"You okay bud? You look shocked," I said as we both laughed.

"Bro, I almost shit myself! I've never been caught up in indirect fire."

"Yeah man, it's Iraq. It happens," I said.

Fortunately for the Secret Service, DS agents serving in Iraq and our contractor colleagues are all too familiar with IDF; so, in turn, we were there to protect them too.

IDF in Baghdad was a weekly occurrence. Sometimes rockets were launched at us several times a day. The timing of this one, however, was a bit suspicious. Just as VP Biden exited the Ambassador's residence, rockets begin flying in? C'mon. Other agents and I think that someone in that house made a phone call or sent a text message about the VP's whereabouts in an attempt to target him. It makes perfect sense. The IDF began flying right around the time the ECMs were shut off. But, that's all speculation.

IDF was so common in Baghdad that we rarely heard about it in the news. The embassy Public Affairs Office (PAO) put out that the rockets never hit the compound and landed in the river. They indicated that the VP was never in danger. Not sure how that mix up occurred. I suspect politics, as that was just a year before the U.S. was scheduled to pull out of Iraq. I can tell you with confidence, however, that anyone on the NEC was in danger from IDF 24/7. The Vice President of the United States, in this instance, was no different. No one can stop a rocket, not even the mighty Secret Service.

Inside a C-130 Hercules about to land at Baghdad International Airport.

Agents Unknown

Damage from one of the IDF rockets that passed over Vice President Biden and landed near the Marine House. The other impact site was just down the road. The velocity of which the concrete flew through the air could easily injure or kill anyone nearby.

Visiting the infamous cross-swords in Baghdad.

About to head up in a Little Bird helicopter to get the layout of the Area of Operations.

CHAPTER 4

SPARTAN 26

Less than one year after my 60-day temporary assignment to Baghdad, I was on a return trip to serve there for a full year tour. This time I was flying to Iraq from Amman, Jordan, and the trip was much more pleasant. I got a lift from my hotel directly to the Queen Alia International Airport. I was met by individuals in neon yellow vests from the Iraq Support Unit, or ISU-Amman. ISU-Amman was there to facilitate our travel on "Embassy Air," which was the U.S. State Department's own air wing. The ISU took us to the check-in desk, walked us through security, and corralled us in our own waiting area. This was service!

After a couple of hours waiting, we boarded the State Department aircraft, a Bombardier Dash-8 TurboProp airplane, through the regular terminal and gate. I took my seat and kicked back. The flight was only going to be a couple of hours. I was ready to get back to do some exciting work.

Shortly after falling asleep, I recall waking up and the plane being about ready to land. I must have slept most of the flight. Upon approach for landing, the Dash-8 didn't conduct any evasive maneuvers. It landed at BIAP just as every other normal aircraft does. I remember wondering if the security situation had changed that much. It hadn't. We were just in a less conspicuous aircraft. Iraq was still a shit show.

Upon arrival at BIAP, the aircraft taxied over to the U.S. military side of the airport. This process seemed all too familiar. I disembarked and made my way over to Sully compound to wait for the Rhino bus. Within a couple of hours, all arriving personnel from Amman, Kuwait, and other areas of Iraq had congregated at Sully compound. The Rhino bus arrived, I boarded the large steel bus, and again, headed down the infamous Route Irish to the NEC in the newly named "International Zone," formerly known as the "Green Zone."

Arriving at the embassy was a familiar experience. I picked up my key and was on my way to my apartment. I was able to get settled quickly. The apartment was empty. My roommate hadn't arrived yet. I took a nap, went to the gym, and after that, chow.

The next day I attended the daily intelligence briefing in the chancery building conference room. The briefing hadn't changed much. Threats here, bad guys there, don't get killed. That type of stuff. After the brief I went over to the RSO office, picked up paperwork, and began my check-in process. It was good to be back. I was excited to get to the POD building and see the guys I had worked with earlier during the year. I was there to, again, be an AIC for protective security details, or PSDs. The same work that I conducted on my temporary assignment.

I saw several familiar faces when I arrived at the POD building. I shook some hands and found my desk. I was assigned to Unit 2.

For the next few weeks, I worked with a number of different PSD teams within Unit 2. All of the teams were designated

"Spartan" teams with a number associated. I was running both high- and low-profile missions into the Red Zone around Baghdad. High-profile details are exactly what it sounds like: high-profile armored Suburbans with large ECMs erected about six feet above the Suburban. Tactically and aggressively, our motorcades moved in unison throughout the streets of Baghdad. Low-profile details used atypical movement tactics to get around the Red Zone. Their vehicles were covert. I'll leave it at that.

I enjoyed working with both types of teams, but I wanted my own team. I was eager to develop a rapport: train, work, feed, and talk shit. I had a lot in common with many of the TC guys. They were all veterans, many of them Marines.

The TC guys lived a much harder life in Baghdad than us direct hires. Unfortunately, some of the guys felt that they were treated like second-class citizens. And, in some cases, they were. They weren't allowed to drink alcohol, and they lived off the embassy compound in some pretty meager digs. They had moved from their beloved "Man Camp" and were now living across the street from the NEC on another USG leased compound. On that compound they lived in a "Chu," or a trailer, rather than an apartment. The Chus generally didn't have any running water, internet was spotty, and there was no overhead cover to protect them from a rocket landing on their trailer.

A few weeks after my arrival, I was assigned to Spartan 2-6. I was pumped. I didn't know any of the guys from 2-6. I had only heard of them, but I was excited to get to know them. As with any team in any environment, being accepted is a process. I had figured this would be the case. I knew the experienced resided within 2-6. I would rely on them heavily. However, I also had my own experiences. I had spent a few months on the ground previously and was ready to begin training and working with them.

The first guy I met was Pedro, the shift leader. Pedro, aka "Cuba," was born and raised in Cuba. He moved to the U.S. and couldn't even speak English yet when he enlisted in the Marine Corps. Cuba had some hilarious stories about his time in boot camp when he didn't understand a thing the drill instructors were saying. Cuba was a former infantry Marine and sniper. He was also a professional mixed martial arts fighter. Cuba had been on the ground in Baghdad for several years. He was extremely humble and perpetually in a good mood. He was well known for his big smile and famous fist bump.

I discussed with Cuba my role within the team. Although all AICs in the POD have specific duties to conduct within their teams, some of the AICs were lazy and did not do their portion of the work. Unfortunately, some of them would put this burden on the contractors who had enough work to do. I wasn't about that. I was there to work and do my part, so that's what I did.

I told Cuba I wanted to train with the team. I asked him to let me know of any training iterations they were going to be conducting. As an AIC, I was responsible for the PAX, or passengers. Generally, the protocol was to meet with the PAX the day before their trip into the Red Zone. I would gather details of their trip, ensure they coordinated with their point of contact (POC) at the venue, ask the purpose of their meeting, and if the meeting would be contentious. I asked these questions because sometimes trips would get approved by our TOC, but the PAX had no business going out into the Red Zone. I didn't want to take my team into harm's way just so an individual could have tea and baklava with a friend. It happened regularly with other teams, but I investigated more thoroughly to mitigate most of those issues with 2-6.

I also told Cuba I wanted to be involved in the planning. This meant reviewing routes and personnel management. I wanted to ensure oversight but also let him know that I gave a shit. I was never there to micromanage Cuba or the team. He knew my intent, and I let him know that I trusted him. Rarely did I overrule any of the plans he made. As the AIC of the team, however, I was ultimately responsible for the actions of the team and could be held accountable in the event of a catastrophe. I wanted to have a comprehensive understanding of our internal team operations so that if something bad did happen, I could clearly articulate our responses. Cuba was cool with it. I think he was happy that he had an AIC that showed interest.

Other members of the team were veterans of both the military and Triple Canopy. Most of them had served in the Marines or Army and just about all of them had served in combat. That is valuable experience to have when serving on a protection detail in Iraq. I'm gonna take the time to introduce these guys because they deserve it.

Matt Rawls, aka Sleepy, was one of the first guys I was able to have a conversation with. Sleepy is a former Force Reconnaissance Marine, a former Sam Houston State Quarterback, and a very talented musician. He also trained in mixed martial arts. He stands about 6'4" tall with sleeve tattoos on his arm and tattoos on his torso that come up his back to his neck. He had the World Trade Center on fire tattooed on his body and looked like he was perpetually ready to fuck shit up. I was glad to have him on my side. I remember standing outside a door at the "Clock Tower," one of our more common venues just outside the embassy walls with Sleepy and asking him some questions. I had just left Houston, and he was from Texas. I figured why not build a rapport, but I'm not sure he was having it.

"Matt, you from Texas, right?"

"Yup," he said with a big dip in his mouth.

"Cool. I just left Houston."

He just nodded.

"Where you from in Texas?" I added.

"Houston area," he said as he scanned the room.

"You get back often?"

"When I can."

Ahh, a man of many words Sleepy was. Soon Cuba came by and rescued Sleepy. Good talk, I thought. Sleepy took a while to crack, but once he did, I knew he had my back. Later that year, we celebrated the Marine Corps birthday together. We shut that place down and walked out drinking, each from our own bottles of red wine.

Rod, a former Marine and Army Airborne Infantry guy, was quick on my radar. I remember our first training iteration. We were conducting arrivals and departures at venues. This means we were practicing getting in and out of armored Suburbans and walking into a "venue." This is one of the most important parts of protection in Iraq as the protectee is no longer inside an armored shell but, instead, out in the open. On departure training, I thought it was a good idea for our primary protectee, the higher ranking individual, to get inside the closest door of the Suburban when departing the building. It was against protocol taught in training; usually the highest level protectee sits in the back seat on the passenger side. My thought was, "why expose an individual to more threats by taking them around the Suburban to a passenger side?" A good idea in theory, but Rod brought up a good point. If someone was shooting from that side, we should abandon that plan and check to the furthest door. An open door on the driver side could lead to a bullet hitting the driver in the head, then we're really fucked. True. I conceded that under "contact," being shot at, we'd revert back to our initial training and go to the far side door. Generally, Rod was a pretty quiet dude. When he did get involved in the training or shit talk in our team, his quick wit and sarcastic comebacks were a force to be reckoned with. Rod, another good ol' boy from Texas, could squat and deadlift all the weights in the gym; it was good to have him on our side.

George Grant, yet another former Marine, was the most refined of all team members. That's not to disparage the other guys; he just took more pride in his eloquent execution of the English language. He too had a quick wit. George's personality was more congenial than most of the other guys on the team, including myself. He was the perpetual diplomat, always charismatic and charming, and had a knack for being extremely well organized. His handsomeness was only superseded by his intellect. I have no doubt, however, that given a situation, he would also fuck shit up.

Bryan, aka Mongoose, was the lone Army Special Forces Soldier on the team. Quiet, humble, and "operator as fuck," Bryan mostly kept to himself unless he had something vital to say. Bryan was one of the hardest workers on the team. He was respected by all, in particular me. He started his own operation making tactical gear: holsters, magazine holders, tactical belts, and more. Bryan wore his own gear on our missions and even provided some to the team members. I didn't get any, although he promised me some. Still waiting, Mongoose! He was always one step ahead tactically and was a major asset to our team.

Alfonso Matos was a former infantry Marine and a beast of men. He was a hard worker, and his tough talkin' Dominican tone would intimidate most opponents who dared to step to him. Matos, also a former Marine, stood about 6'3" tall and around 240 lbs. He walked, talked, and sounded like Mr. T. I remember my first encounter with Matos was on that same training iteration with Rod. The dude was motivated. I was immediately impressed with his tenacity but was certain that he'd kill someone who looked at our protectee the wrong way. Matos was explained by Rod as "a person of extremes." If he had your back, he had it full speed ahead, and there was no stopping him. Matos was a warrior and had the scars to prove it. He was hit by an IED while in the Marine Corps; his body badly mangled. He still has the large scar on his leg. Not to be fucked with, Matos feared nothing.

Alex, the Russian assassin, was one of the more quiet dudes on the team. He was promoted to the tactical commander for the team once Cuba left, and he was damn good at it. A former U.S. Army Ranger, Alex was as deadly as he was silent. I had met Alex briefly on my previous tour to Iraq. I remember meeting him, hearing his accent, and calling him "Sasha," a nickname for Alex in Russian. He wasn't too impressed. I never called him Sasha again. Alex's brother also served in the military and with TC. Both born in Russia, humble and proud, they dedicated their lives to serving the U.S. I'd want no one other than Alex leading us around the streets of Baghdad.

Sean, aka Doc, was a former Army Ranger as well. He rivaled George's handsomeness. He too was a large man. Sean was so amiable I often felt like an asshole for my lack of articulacy and foul language. Which one of us was the diplomat? Doc was sometimes referred to as "Optimus Prime," in reference to the *Transformers* movie because he was always doing the right thing. I knew I could count on him. Doc and I spent a lot of time together. As the team medic, we worked hand-in-hand; wherever the protectee went and wherever I went, he went. He was always respectful and courteous and a funny dude in his own right. I couldn't have asked for a better teammate to stand outside of meetings in Iraqi ministry buildings as feces filled the air. Doc became one of my closest friends on the team, and he still is today.

Jason Jarvis, another Marine, served as the "limo" driver throughout my time in Baghdad. This means I rode in the passenger seat next to him. He was soft spoken and perpetually jovial. He was an extremely hard worker and a dedicated team member. I could count on him for anything. Jason had the task of making everything around our protectee seem pleasant. No matter how much chaos surrounded us in the streets of Baghdad, Jason kept order as if on a smooth ride to the ball. I never heard Jason complain about a thing, even though we were often put in some shitty situations. Jason was a black belt in taekwondo, a purple heart recipient, and a ninja at driving an armored Suburban through the mangled streets of Baghdad smoothly. His driving spoiled me. I was lucky to have him.

The team was made up of more members who rotated in and out, but the guys mentioned here are those that I was, and still am, closest with.

Within a couple months of my arrival, Spartan 2-6 was scheduled for a mission to setup security at a venue in advance of the protectees arrival. I attended the intelligence brief before our mission and learned that previous day there was a large Vehicle Borne Improvised Explosive Device (VBIED) attack in a local market. We had been warned of the increased volatility and that attacks were on the rise. This had an effect on what routes our motorcade would take to the venues. We had to pay special attention to stay away from those routes and the areas of recent explosions.

VBIEDs and IEDs were common in the city. There were several a day, and although they weren't always aimed at U.S. motorcades, we were still the prime target for Iranian Backed Militias (IBM). During this time, Baghdad was unofficially partitioned into different sects throughout the city. The Sunni and Shia were continuing their struggle that had begun thousands of years ago. Saddam Hussein, a Sunni, oppressed the Shias during his reign. Now, the new Prime Minister Nouri Al-Maliki, a Shia, was surrounding himself with his Shia allies and thus suppressing the Sunnis that had previously reigned supreme.

Iraq's neighbor Iran, also a Shia Muslim nation, had a significant influence on the dynamics inside Iraq at this time. In particular, they were suspected of supporting Muqtada Al-Sadr, a popular Shia cleric and leader of his own militia. As Rod put it, Baghdad had an "insidious Iranian influence that had become more and more brazen thanks to a weak central government. The city had essentially been sliced up into smaller fiefdoms." Rod speaks truth. By far, the majority of the IEDs or VBIEDs throughout the city were a direct result of the sectarian violence. The attacks that were conducted against Sunnis were usually executed by IBMs.

None of this, however, really mattered at the moment. We had a job to do, and the mission was still on. While Spartan 2-6 was generally a "movement team," or a team that provided protection for an individual, on this day we were the advance team. Before the mission, we had a team briefing at our motorcade, also known as a "hood brief." The hood brief was to review all of our assignments, ensure we all knew the mission, the rules of engagement, emergency response plans, and double check our loadout.

Prior to the hood brief, I was notified that one of the other Spartan teams was redirected on their route and had been sent back to the NEC. They could not complete their mission. I remember calling the TOC to get an update. The TOC noted that some of the streets were shut down due to the previous day's attack. Our mission was still on. It was deemed "critical," although every mission into the Red Zone was allegedly critical.

Spartan 2-6 departed the international zone checkpoint in a four-vehicle motorcade made up of armored Suburbans. Inside the lead vehicle was Sleepy as the driver, the tactical commander, and our PPS, Saker. The K-9 vehicle was second. I sat in the passenger seat with Jason as the driver and two K9 handlers in the back with their dog. The Emergency Response Vehicle, or ERV, was the third vehicle in the motorcade with George as the driver, the medic in the passenger seat, and Mongoose in the rear. Unfortunately, Sean wasn't available for this movement, so we had another medic. And, lastly, was the follow vehicle where the shift leader Larry sat. Cuba was out on break. I knew Larry from my TDY in Baghdad the previous year. He was one of the most experienced shift leaders in Baghdad. Matos and Rod were the shooters in the back of the follow. Matos brought along a M249 SAW machine gun, and Rod brought a sniper rifle. All team members were carrying a Glock 17 9mm pistol and a M4 carbine assault rifle; all with multiple magazines and personal protective equipment that included helmet, tactical vests with armored plates, and a medical kit.

Shortly after departure, the lead vehicle called an audible on the routes. Just as reported in the intel brief, the recent attacks caused random street closures, and snap checkpoints were popping up everywhere. We had to find a different way to the venue. A snap checkpoint is a checkpoint set up at random by the local security apparatus. Usually checkpoints were set up by the Iraqi Army (IA), but some smaller checkpoints were set up by the local Iraqi police (IP). We never truly knew what would happen at checkpoints; the IA and IPs were paid very little and had minimal training. This meant that they could easily be paid off to cap an American if needed. To exacerbate our concerns, we learned earlier that week that IA and IP uniforms had been stolen and sold on the black market. This made it even more precarious; we really didn't know who was manning these checkpoints.

After a few minutes on the new route, our lead vehicle called out a snap checkpoint over the radio. The motorcade slowly came to a halt when Saker opened the back door of the lead Suburban and showed the police our placard. The placards are created by the U.S. Embassy and signed by the Iraqi Ministry of Foreign Affairs (MOFA). It approved us to conduct our duties as a diplomatic PSD throughout Baghdad. Or at least that's what it was supposed to do.

I had immediate concerns as we stopped. The checkpoint location put us in a perilous situation as our motorcade blocked traffic behind us. This incited anger in the local Iraqi drivers. The way the traffic cop aggressively snatched the placard out of Saker's hand was also telling of what was to come. The traffic cop walked away with the the placard and showed it to an IP and an IA soldier. They chatted for longer than generally necessary, so Saker exited the vehicle and approached them. The police initially dismissed him, but within seconds, the cop turned to Saker and the conversation became more volatile. Our tactical commander exited the vehicle to see what was going on. The situation continued to intensify as the police became more antagonistic with their arm gestures and shouting. I began to crack my door, and as I did so, I noticed Larry walk by. No doubt he had been through something like this before, and he was masterful at deescalating in these situations. As Larry deployed out of the vehicle, so did Rod and Matos on both the left and right sides of the follow vehicle. Bryan and the medic also deployed outside of the ERV and took up positions.

As Larry approached, I heard one of the guys on the radio, "Keep your eyes open, boys." Something didn't feel right. The checkpoint was littered with authorities in different uniforms: traffic police, local police, and Iraqi Army. That didn't make sense to us. Usually, it is just one entity that manages these checkpoints. Keeping in mind that Iraqi police and Army uniforms had been reported stolen, and the information that terrorists could use these in a surprise attack, we were all on edge. Furthermore, the dynamics at this checkpoint were different than most. Sure, we were held up at checkpoints before, but the cops generally treated us with more civility than this. These guys seemed like they were picking a fight.

As Rod scanned his sector, he noticed a half-built multi-story building to the right of the motorcade. There were some people on top of that building that looked up to no good. "I have movement in these houses on the right," Rod said. Matos was on the left side scanning his sector where there was a wall lining the street. At the end of that wall was a DShK, a Soviet-made heavy machine gun mounted on a vehicle. That vehicle had boxed us in, and the DShK was pointed right at our motorcade. Matos replied, "Roger, I got a DShk on the left."

I remember the intensity of the teams radio traffic. I noticed the vehicle traffic around us start to slow to almost none at all.

I said to Jason, "Traffic is slowing on both sides of the road. Something isn't right."

The K-9 handlers and Jarvis agreed.

"Jason, that was Grey 85 we just passed, right?"

"Yes, sir." I was referring to one of our Grey codes or "way points."

I got on the radio to call Spartan base, which is the call sign for the radio operator in the TOC. For reference, AICs rarely get on the radio. Generally, when we have protectee in our vehicle, we listen to the radio traffic of the team and will only interject if we need to. We also keep the doors "buttoned up," or locked, to mitigate anyone trying to get in or out. But this time was different. We had no protectee. Larry could no longer reach Spartan base from his handheld radio, so I took over the communications.

"Spartan Base, Spartan 2-6..." I said.

"Go ahead 2-6."

"Be advised. We're approximately 500 meters north of Grey 85. — We're static at a snap checkpoint."

Being static is never good. PSDs always want to be moving until we arrive at our location. It makes for a harder target. Get off and stay off the "X."

As Spartan base began to reply, Larry came on the mic.

"Hey, Cody. They wanna look inside our motorcade."

"Negative, that's not gonna happen," I said.

"Roger that," he replied. Larry knew we weren't gonna approve a search of the motorcade. I think he radioed me just to let the police think he was checking.

"Be advised. I'm on the net with base," I said.

"Copy."

A couple minutes went by, and Spartan base called again, "Spartan 2-6, what's your status?

"Base, 2-6, still static. IPs took our placard. We're trying to get it back." Silence over the net for a few seconds. Then Spartan base called again.

"2-6, do you need support?"

"Base, 2-6, yeah go ahead and stand up QRF. I'll let you know if we need 'em."

"2-6, copy, standing up QRF."

We were all anxious as we scanned our sectors and heard the QRF shift leader on the radio confirm the order to "stand up."

Several tense minutes later, Spartan base called again, "Spartan 2-6, this is base."

"Base, go for 2-6."

"The HIRRT team is mobile and conducting training in the area. Would you like them to do a fly by?"

The HIRRT team was the U.S. Embassies Helicopter Insertion Rapid Response Team. Their primary mission was to rescue any of the PSDs that needed support out in the Red Zone. It was headed up by one DS special agent and TC guys as shooters—the same makeup as the PSD teams. The HIRRT guys flew in two Bell-UH 1 helicopters, better known as "Hueys." They were usually hanging out the door of the Hueys with their feet just above the skids. They wore khaki flight suits, tactical gear, and had rifles. They appeared intimidating to anyone on the ground.

I paused for a second and thought of the potential ramifications. If the HIRRT team did a fly by, this may frighten the police into letting us go. Conversely, it could piss these police off enough or even startle them to the point of engaging us in a firefight.

"Fuck it," I said to Jarvis. "We need to get moving." I approved the fly-by." Roger that base, have HIRRT buzz the checkpoint."

Moments later I could hear the rotors of the Hueys on approach. "Spartan Base, be advised. I have a visual on Spartan 2-6," I heard over the radio from the HIRRT shift leader. Then I saw one of the Hueys in front of me. It banked hard and low on the left side of our motorcade right over the checkpoint. After doing so, the Huey pulled up and came around to make another run. Another Huey was circling up above. I could see the uneasy look on the face of the police and soldiers as they looked up at the men with guns in the helicopter circling above.

"Spartan base we're gonna maintain a visual," the HIRRT team shift leader said.

Spartan base relayed the information to me, "2-6, this is base. HIRRT has your visual. They'll remain on site."

"Base, 2-6, roger. I have a visual."

Within minutes, maybe even seconds, of the HIRRT team buzzing our location, they were coming back for another fly by. I saw the look of discomfort come across the face of the traffic cop. The Huey lowered to make the second fly by and buzz the checkpoint; the cop quickly handed the placard to Saker, hurriedly walked away, and waved us on. The plan worked. "Base, 26, be advised. They've handed us back the placard. We'll be mobile soon." Larry and the guys got back in the motorcade. "2-6, let's roll," Larry said as we departed.

The remainder of our trip to the venue was uneventful. When we did finally arrive, all of the team members were trying to figure out what the hell just happened. We all knew that something didn't feel right. I asked Saker to come over and brief me. Saker told me he thought it was the Iraqi intelligence unit. What was unique about that scenario was that the chain of command was off. The traffic police, who usually wield no power whatsoever, were in charge of the checkpoint. The IP was there as an observer; and the IA, who usually has the most authority, was last in the reporting structure and seemed indifferent. If this was Iraqi intelligence, their tradecraft was shit.

In Iraq motorcades generally encounter some type of resistance on just about every mission. But this one was different. We knew Iraqi Army and Police uniforms were stolen and the command structure of this motley crew didn't make sense. In that moment we also noticed the traffic start to slow and an eerily quiet come over the area. When the locals disappear from a busy street, that is usually an indicator that some type of attack is about to pop off.

The movement team, who we were setting up security for, although delayed because of our checkpoint shenanigans, arrived to the venue without issue. Once they were secure on venue, we loaded up and made our way back to the embassy compound with relative ease. I was asked by my boss to report to him and tell him about our incident. I also wanted to get information from our intelligence unit in the TOC. I asked the team to meet in the chancery conference room after they dropped their gear so we could debrief after I spoke to the bosses.

I was told by the TOC that Iraqi Intelligence Units were cracking down on embassy PSDs and trying to gather intelligence on what type of weapons we were carrying because of the large VBIED the day before. That didn't make sense. Why would they look into us? We didn't blow shit up. Typical in Iraq, rarely did anything make sense.

Later that day, we learned that a U.S. Army convoy had been hit by an IED in that same location. That made us all wonder about our previous situation and if we were their initial targets. We may have dodged a catastrophe. But who was doing this? Was the Iraqi Intelligence Unit trying to set us up to get hit? The "new" Iraqi government was primarily Shia, so was Iran, and so was Muqtada Al-Sadr. Were they working together? The conspiracy theories flowed through my mind and the minds of the team.

I personally think that we were targeted, but the hard men of Spartan 2-6 scared the terrorists away with our war faces. Seriously though, that was a close call, and we all knew it. We would never know for sure why we were held up at that checkpoint. Just another day in Iraq.

I remember getting back to my apartment that night and Facetiming home with my parents. My sister was there also. I was drinking a Scotch. I didn't say a word about the incident, but they knew something was up.

My sister said, "What's up, lil bro? You ok?"

"Yeah, I'm good, Sis."

Mom could tell something was up too, so she began to ask questions.

"It was nothing, Mom. Just calling to say hi," and I left it at that.

I learned later from the guys that that may have been a watershed moment when they began to trust me. They thought the decisions I made to get on the radio, stand up the QRF, and ultimately, have the HIRRT buzz our locations were good decisions. The team and I began to grow closer as time passed. We trained together more, spent more time in shitty Baghdad ministries, refugee camps outside of Sadr city, and taxiing around Congressional Delegations. Some of us hung out together at Baghdaddys, and on occasion, I'd have them over to my apartment when my roommate was out. I cooked gumbo, and we kicked back some beers.

I left Baghdad in April of 2012. Before leaving, the guys threw me a small gathering at the outdoor pool. We played some cornhole, did some swimming, sunned our manly physiques, and BBQ'd. The guys presented me with a subdued black and grey American flag with a Spartan Helmet and under it read "Spartan 26." The guys signed the back of the flag and left me some love notes. But, best of all, I was handed a sheet of paper with a picture on it. It was a picture of Scott's Selection Single Malt Liquor 1977, a 35-year-aged bottle of Scotch. Rod said, "This will be waiting for you when you get home." That meant a lot to me.

The camaraderie and friendships I made that year working with Spartan 2-6 were some of the best of my career. It is on par with some of the relationships I built in the Marine Corps. When times are shitty, bonds are formed. This time in Iraq was no different. I am still in touch with most of the guys today—all of which are successful in their careers, have expanded their families, and continue to do big things. I am proud to call the men of Spartan 2-6 one of the best group of dudes I've ever worked with. I am honored to call them friends.

Protecting Congressional Delegation (CODEL) Dreier as they meet with U.S. military leaders in Baghdad. Pictured here: David Dreier (R-CA) at the Suburban door and Keith Ellison (D-MN) shaking hands.

Agents Unknown

Spartan 26 at the United States Marine Corps Ball celebrating our 236th Birthday.
Pictured from left to right: Jason, Cody, George, Matt, Sean, Cuba.

Farewell from Spartan 26.
Pictured from left to right: Jason, Alfonso, Cody, Alex, Rod (face blurred) Bryan, George.

CHAPTER 5

A MILLION DOLLAR FRAUD

As my flight from Tokyo-Narita airport circled the runway, a sense of thrill and excitement overcame me. I stared down at the rice fields below me and imagined the history that took place here: the war, the politics, and the subsequent controversies all intrigued me so much. I was about to land in one of the most notorious countries I'd heard of as a child: Vietnam. It was June of 2012, and I was arriving to serve at the U.S. Consulate in Ho Chi Minh City, otherwise known as Saigon, for a two-year assignment. Saigon was one of my top choices to serve in after leaving Baghdad. Being that it was centrally located in Southeast Asia, it was only an hour or so flight to some of the most tropical destinations on earth: Bali, Koh Samui, Phuket. Good food, great people, and a rich history. I couldn't wait to be on the ground.

Upon arrival I disembarked the plane and hurriedly walked towards the Vietnam immigration desks. I wanted to get there before the long lines began. As I arrived to the diplomatic line at customs and immigrations, I smiled to the customs agent and said hello. He just looked at me with no emotion, stamped my passport, and waved me on. I made my way down the escalator, and I saw a familiar face. It was Derek, a fellow DS agent and friend. Derek and I had known each other for a couple of years. We met in Houston when he had come to work on a big fraud case he was investigating. I was glad to see him. We grabbed my bags and exited the airport to the consulate van. I shook hands with the driver, and we were on our way.

The city was bustling with bicycles, motorbikes, and taxis. There appeared to be no traffic laws. Motorbikes zoomed in and out of traffic at a high rate of speed as if it were against the law to go any slower. Motorbikes with one, two, three, and sometimes four people on it were common. I was surprised when I did not see even one crash on my trip. A controlled chaos is what it was.

Saigon was humid, especially this time of year. It reminded me of summers in Louisiana. When stepping outside, the humidity felt like a mist hitting me in the face.

I had traveled to Ho Chi Minh City alone as I had in all my assignments. I remember arriving to the Somerset Hotel and Apartments: my new home for the next two years. The Somerset was on the corner of Nguyen Thi Minh Khai and Mac Dinh Chi Street—right in the heart of the city. My apartment on the 13th floor was a three bedroom and about 1,700 square feet. As I walked out onto the patio, I looked down and could see an olympic-size pool with chairs and people sunbathing. Just beyond that pool was the U.S. Consulate compound. When I submitted my request to the Housing Board, I said I wanted to be close to the consulate. They didn't mess around. I was basically right on top of it.

I went to bed early that night and woke up around 0430. Jet lag was awful. The sun began to rise around 0500, so I decided to go for a run to familiarize myself with the area. I stretched a bit near the entrance of the Somerset and noticed there was a lot of traffic. I also noticed some Vietnamese people on motorbikes staring at me. Some were waving; some were laughing. I figured they thought I was crazy to be up so early for a run. I learned later they were just amused at the big bearded white man with tattoos. I humored them and waved back. I started on my run and went for what I thought was about three miles. When I left the Somerset, I felt I had a good grasp on the location as I identified a very tall building as a good landmark. But in the midst of dodging motorbikes, pedestrians, and food carts, I could no longer see that building. I was lost for the next thirty minutes or so until I ended up near the front gates of the consulate. I walked back from there, past the local guards who would soon be part of my team.

Later that morning, Derek met me in front of Somerset and we made our way to the consulate. The boss Craig was just arriving to the consulate. I shook his hand and met with him for a few minutes. Craig was a seasoned special agent with about fifteen years on the job. He had served at multiple overseas assignments previously and had a good name in DS. He carried the title Regional Security Officer, and I was to be his deputy. Craig had a perpetual serious look on his face. As time passed, he couldn't resist my country accent and corny jokes. I'd frequently get a smile out of him.

Derek's role in the Regional Security Office was different than mine. Whereas my role would be overseeing day-to-day security operations, his role was almost exclusively investigations.

He served in a position that DS calls an "ARSO-I," or Assistant Regional Security Officer-Investigator. He investigated visa fraud at the consulate, facilitated international fugitive returns, and served as the liaison with the local police. Both Derek and I fell under the management and purview of the RSO, Craig.

After my short meeting with Craig, I spent the remainder of the morning completing paperwork and finishing up the check-in process. Later that afternoon, Derek took me down to the consular section to meet a guy named Mark. Mark was also a single dude, and Derek thought we'd get along well. Mark stood up to shake my hand, and we chatted a bit. He was a former U.S. Marshal and current reservist in the Navy. We had enough in common, and I thought this guy may be alright to hang out with.

Not like I had much choice though. When serving in a tight-knit diplomatic community overseas, people tend to be drawn to those who are in similar situations as them. Families hang out with families, couples with couples, and singles with singles. The limited amount of people at some posts further exacerbates these situations where there may only be one or two single people to go to restaurants, bars, cafes, travel, or to just explore with. This was my issue when I arrived in Ho Chi Minh City. Mark was one of the only single guys.

I began hanging with Mark a couple times a week. He wanted to go out more frequently, but I just wasn't into it. I found myself a rhythm of waking up early to work out. I joined a gym, California Fitness and Yoga Club, and it opened at 0600. I'd take a taxi in the mornings at first, then ride my bicycle, then finally graduated to riding my 110cc Harley—I mean, Honda Wave.

Mark stood about 6'3" tall with kind of a hunchback, small glasses, and short hair. Mark was not well liked in the consulate.

I did not know how people felt about him until later though. He seemed OK to me. He was friendly and polite. The kind of dude that jumps in the front seat of the taxi, pulls the seat up so you have enough room, and then pays the taxi fare. Actually, he did that often. He did his share of paying bar tabs; he picked up the bill for dinner on occasion. He seemed like a decent dude.

I did think it was weird that, one time on a date with a Vietnamese model (he made sure I knew she was a model), he asked me in advance to call him and get him out of the date so that he could go out on another date. I never called. Ain't nobody got time for that. Instead, he called me, said some random shit, and got out of the date on his own.

A couple months went by, and I continued to hang with Mark. We'd go to the Brazilian steakhouse almost every week and eat all the meat one could desire. I'd go with him to different bars and clubs in town. Xu Lounge was one of our favorites. On some mornings, we'd take a break from work and walk over to the Coffee Bean across from the consulate to get some caffeine.

As time passed, I began to see a different side of Mark. In front of Vietnamese people, mainly women, he'd try to embarrass me. His usual "joke" was to tease me because I didn't speak the language. He'd use his Vietnamese language skills to flirt with girls. He always thought he was smarter than everyone else. He'd have business cards handy to pass out to girls in an attempt to impress them. The cards read "Nonimmigrant Visa - Chief" both in English and Vietnamese. Douchebag move I thought. What I found most interesting is when other American diplomats from the consulate were around, he was very quiet. He didn't seem as if he wanted to be around them. I soon learned why. I was hanging with the wrong company and nearly paying dearly for it.

One day while sitting in the Craig's office, Derek came in and eagerly closed the door.

"Craig, I need to talk to you about something. I think this is big," he said.

Craig, being the calm, cool New Yorker looked up at Derek and said, "Have a seat."

Derek began to explain, "We received a 'poison pen' in the mail. It's from a Vietnamese man whose wife was issued a visa illegally. The guy gives details of how she did it, including the description of the 'tall, white man' who issued the visa."

Craig looked perturbed. "Go on," he said.

"I analyzed the information and ran some checks. It's leading back to the Nonimmigrant Visa Chief, Mark. I need to conduct some more research, but I feel confident something is going on."

Craig told Derek to continue his investigation and report back his results. And Derek would. Derek was one of the most talented investigators I've ever worked with in DS. He was a bulldog: aggressive, well organized, and skilled. If the information on that letter was true, Derek would find out.

A poison pen letter is a letter written from an anonymous individual that usually gives information of some type of malicious or illegal activity. Most of the time they are just some crazy person talking nonsense. Generally, because of the sheer number of poison pens that are shit, they are often overlooked. This one, fortunately for us, was not taken lightly and fell into Derek's hands.

So what is a Nonimmigrant Visa Chief? It is an individual that oversees the issuance of visas to the United States. U.S. Embassies and Consulates are made up of several sections that each hold their own specific job duties. Just as the RSO section is responsible for security, the Consular section at U.S. diplomatic facilities have their own responsibilities. Consular Services at a U.S. Consulate issue visas, both immigrant and nonimmigrant, to the United States.

For those of you who are unfamiliar with the process of a foreigner visiting or immigrating to America, I will explain. In order for foreigners to visit the U.S., they must apply for a "visa," which is a permit to enter. Visa applications are reviewed by consular officers at embassies and consulates abroad. These consular officers have the authority to deny or approve visas based on a number of stipulations and circumstances. They are very well trained and have a comprehensive understanding of the different types of visas, requirements, and disqualifying information that could prevent an individual from entering the U.S.

Not all countries have a visa requirement if only wishing to enter the U.S. just for a visit. Friendly countries to the U.S.—for example, the United Kingdom, Australia and many other countries—do not need a visa to visit as long as they do not plan to remain in the U.S. indefinitely. This is part of what the U.S. calls its "Visa Waiver Program."[3] Usually 90 days is the limit, but each type of nonimmigrant visa is different. Some examples of nonimmigrant visas are business visas, visitor visas, work visas, student visas, performing athletes visas, and more. If, however, an individual plans to move to the U.S. and reside there

---

3 "Apply for Nonimmigrant Visas to the U.S," https://www.usa.gov/visas#item-213289.

permanently, no matter which country that individual is from, then they must apply for an "immigrant" visa.[4]

Low-income immigrants from third world countries have a harder time obtaining a visa to the United States. Those who do make it to the U.S. could find overstaying their approved time in the United States more appealing than returning to their home country at their visas expiration. Because of the overwhelming number of individuals from third world countries seeking entrance into the U.S. and the amount of individuals that overstay their visas, consular officers must scrutinize these applications very closely in an attempt to eliminate fraudulent applications, dishonest applicants, and those who show indicators that they might remain in the U.S. after their visa expires.

The Vietnamese fall into this category. It is extremely difficult for a Vietnamese citizen to obtain a nonimmigrant visa just to visit the U.S. and even harder to obtain a visa to live in the U.S. permanently. Therefore, having someone on the inside that can help facilitate the issuance of a visa is a huge advantage for local Vietnamese. A Vietnamese citizen might pay their whole life savings to have this opportunity.

This is where Mark and his position of authority was manipulated. As the NIV Chief, he was the boss of the NIV section. The consular officers worked for him. Mark had the power to overturn consular officers decisions. So, for example, if an individual was denied a visa to the United States by a consular officer, Mark could and would, for the right amount of money, make sure the denial was overturned. The Vietnamese citizen would get the visa, and Mark would subsequently get paid.

---

[4] "Directory of Visa Categories," https://travel.state.gov/content/travel/en/us-visas/visa-information-resources/all-visa-categories.html.

As Derek began to investigate further, he learned that this was going to be a monumental endeavor. Investigating a case of this magnitude needed patience, determination, and more assets. DS Headquarters (HQ) was notified, and they put an agent from the Criminal Fraud Investigations, or CFI, unit in charge of the case. CFI had numerous amounts of resources at their disposal. They handled the largest fraud cases worldwide and have nearly unlimited reach. The agents in CFI are very good at what they do. The plan was for Derek to run the show on the ground in Ho Chi Minh City, at the direction of a special agent named Scott from CFI.

Now that DS HQ had a handle on things, I asked Derek how HQ wanted me to handle my "relationship" with Mark. To just stop hanging with him would surely make him suspicious. To keep hanging with him would make me look suspicious. HQ came back and advised that I keep things as normal as possible but try to minimize how much I hang out with him. Great advice; clear as mud.

I tried my best, but he still contacted me. I recall him sending me a cryptic email one day asking me to come down to the consular section for a security matter. I called him and asked what was up. That was Mark's "cool guy," covert way of telling me a group of Vietnamese models were in the NIV section. I promptly forwarded that email and every email I received from him to Scott from that point on.

Mark would ask me to go out, but I was too tired. He'd ask me to go to coffee, but I was too busy. He'd come to my office, and all of a sudden, I had to be somewhere. The community was so damn small, it was hard to escape this guy! But the biggest challenge for me was yet to come. Mark, a guy named Kevin, a

DS agent friend named Vaughn (who was a mutual friend of all of us), and I had all purchased tickets to Bangkok for Kevin's bachelor party. I remember ruminating over this day in and day out. I went into Craig's office.

"Boss, I can't do it. I don't feel comfortable going."

"It's up to you, Cody. You already bought the ticket though. It could look suspicious if you dropped out."

Derek felt the same, "Man, he's gonna think we're on to him."

We decided that it was best that I don't cancel the trip. Craig, Derek, Scott, and DS HQ knew I was going, so I figured by notifying them, I was covered. I also talked at length with Vaughn, who knew about the investigation of Mark. Vaughn also didn't feel comfortable traveling with him. But Vaughn and Kevin were best friends. He was Kevin's best man. He had to go, and I wasn't gonna leave him hanging.

We traveled to Bangkok to support Kevin, but the trip turned out to be a dud. This is mainly because Vaughn and I did everything we could to stay away from Mark. By staying away from Mark, we had to stay away from Kevin. I know Kevin thought we were being weird, but what were we to do? The guy was being investigated on major federal fraud charges. He was manipulative and betrayed our trust. We're fucking federal agents, and he's doing that under our nose. He was the biggest turd on the turd wagon as far as I was concerned.

Derek and Scott's investigation took precedence over just about any other duties they had. Derek worked on this case every day, often times until late in the evening. It consumed him. But both their hard work paid off. They soon discovered who Mark was working with and a ring of co-conspirators helping him facilitate this fraud. Most of them were American-Vietnamese, some living in the U.S. and some in Vietnam. Scott secured more subpoenas and warrants for their emails, phone records, and anything else one can imagine. Derek and Scott poured over documents, IP addresses, and other data. Mark had been up to this for many months. There was a lot of information to be uncovered.

Mark's plan, though, was not so sophisticated. The investigation revealed a story of lies, deceit, and manipulation. We learned that upon Mark's arrival in country, he befriended an individual named Ben. Ben saw Mark as a target of opportunity: a goofy, lonely American Diplomat in a position of power, in a country filled with beautiful women. Ben furthered his relationship with Mark by introducing him to women, inviting him to fancy dinners, high-profile events, and making him feel special. He even laughed at Mark's jokes. That's absurd. Mark wasn't funny.

Eventually, Ben would pitch his grand idea to Mark. Initially, he just asked Mark to help him out with a visa for a friend who had been previously denied. Ben knew Mark had the authority to overturn the denial and offered to pay Mark a nominal fee if he did. Mark complied and ensured that Ben's friend got a visa. Mark subsequently got paid.

What started as a one-time small deal flourished into a much larger fraud scheme. Eventually, Mark would meet Ben in different locations, sometimes the Coffee Bean across the street, and Ben would hand him a list of five to ten applicants who had a current application for a visa. Many of the applicants had been denied, some not even adjudicated yet, but Mark would see to it that the individuals on that list were approved.

For each individual approved, Mark would receive a 5k to 10k cut. What was interesting is that for each visa issued, Ben was making anywhere from 25k to 75k. The plot also revealed how the money was funneled through a bank in China and into Thailand. Scott did his best to keep track of the flow of money.

In May 2013 a federal arrest warrant was issued for Mark. His tour at the consulate in Ho Chi Minh City had ended. He was supposed to go to Afghanistan for a tour as a reservist with the Navy, but Scott worked with the Department of Defense to make sure that didn't happen. The Navy advised Mark that they were having issues with his clearance. So what did Mark do? He went to Thailand.

On May 13th Mark was walking on a dark street in Phuket, Thailand. Derek was watching him and was emailing Craig and I on his Blackberry.

"I see him. He's walking alone on the street," Derek said. "Just waiting for the police to get him."

Mark was walking with his head down by himself when, suddenly, Thai Police jumped out of a van and grabbed him. They put him in handcuffs and threw him in the van. Derek watched it all go down.

"We got him," Derek emailed. It was over.

The next day Craig and I were in his office, both in a jovial mood after the successful arrest operation. We had to close the door and keep our excitement to a minimum because no one else in the consulate knew of the investigation. Not even the Consul General. We knew we'd soon be answering some questions once word of Mark's arrest got out. And the word did get out, rapidly.

I was in a downstairs office when Craig came running down. He was out of breath. "Cody, they know! Let's go!" The Consul General had called Craig in his office to discuss Mark's arrest. Craig knew I wanted to be there when the news was shared. I ran up the stairs behind Craig, and we made our way into the Consul General's office. Tom, Mark's former boss and one of the few people who liked Mark, was also there. Tom thought Mark was a stellar performer. He gave him an outstanding employee evaluation review. Poor guy, he was going to be shocked.

Tom started, "Mark got arrested in Phuket."

"Yes, I'm aware," said Craig as he slowly nodded his head.

"Really? Do you know why? I figured it was for something with girls," said Tom.

"No, it's not that." Then Craig explained further, "For several months Mark has been under investigation by my office and DS Headquarters"

"For what?" Tom interjected.

"Visa fraud. Mark was selling visas to the Vietnamese."

Tom's face turned red, and his eyes grew large as he threw his hands in the air with a look of astonishment. "What? Are you kidding me? How bad is it?" asked Tom.

"It's bad," Craig said with a very stern look.

I decided to chime in, "Tom, the magnitude of this is..." I struggled for a word, thinking of what I can do to relate the significance of the situation—"inconceivable." I paused for dramatic effect. "We're talking millions of dollars exchanged for visas." Tom just looked at me with a blank stare as his red face turned pale white.

"That's all we can share right now, sir." Craig said to the Consul General. We both walked out of the office leaving them to their imagination.

When Thai police took Mark into custody, they brought him to a Phuket jail. One of the DS agents from the U.S. Embassy in Bangkok joined Derek and the Thai police on the transport to Bangkok days after the arrest. After a couple of days, HQ gave Derek the "OK" to interview Mark. I remember the deafening silence on the audio recording as Derek walked in the room and confronted him.

"Hey, Mark....?" Silence. "Didn't expect to see me, did you?" Derek then went into a very calculated and poignant statement discussing the situation Mark found himself in. Derek laid it all on the table without interruption but then Mark began to ask questions. He asked what would happen to him. Derek couldn't tell him because he didn't know. He just knew Mark was in a lot of trouble, and he articulated that very clearly to him.

After listening to his Miranda Warnings, Mark declined an attorney. He decided it was in his best interest to answer Derek's questions. Derek didn't expect that, but he was prepared. He spilled everything, from beginning to end. Mark named other co-conspirators, discussed the process of the scheme, and told Derek what he did with the money he earned. Derek knew most of it already. Many of the questions he asked were to verify the information already established. Mark was finished. His esteemed career as a Foreign Service Officer was over. His time as a Naval Officer, done.

Within a week Mark was escorted back from Thailand to America by U.S. Marshals. On 06 November 2013, Mark "... plead guilty in the U.S. District for the District of Columbia, to one count each of conspiracy to commit bribery and visa fraud and to defraud the United States, bribery of a public official, and conspiracy to engage in monetary transaction in property derived from illegal activity." [5] On Friday, August 14th, 2015, he was sentenced to 64 months with three years of supervised release after his prison term.

This entire scheme generated at least $9.78 million. Mark "...received over $3 million which he laundered through China and into Thailand. He attempted to hide the illegal proceeds of the scheme by purchasing nine real estate properties in Thailand."[6]

Mark's plan to make millions by defrauding the U.S. government failed horribly. When looking back, Mark met all the indicators of an individual that could be easily manipulated or blackmailed. He was a loner, an introvert, lacked interpersonal skills, and was easily excited by women and the idea of being in power. Ben saw these weaknesses in Mark and took advantage of him. At the time of Mark's arrest, he knew he would endure many years behind bars. The architect of this scheme, Ben, still had his freedoms, likely reading about the arrest in the newspapers. But he wouldn't be free for long. Ben was still living in Vietnam, and we had our eyes on him.

---

5 "Former U.S. Consulate Official Sentenced," https://www.justice.gov/opa/pr/former-us-consulate-official-sentenced-64-months-prison-receiving-over-3-million-bribes.

6 Former U.S. Consulate Official Sentenced," https://www.justice.gov/opa/pr/former-us-consulate-official-sentenced-64-months-prison-receiving-over-3-million-bribes.

Chapter 6

"BEN" THERE, ARRESTED THAT

The reports about Mark's arrest hit the news, and the consulate was abuzz with rumors. How did he do it? Who helped him? Was any other consulate employee involved? There was concern that a local staff member could have been involved; so to determine the magnitude of Mark's nefarious activity, DS sent a team of special agents to interview both local staff and Americans.

There was also speculation about who in the community could have helped Mark. How did he determine who would get a visa? Now that the arrest of Mark was in the news, Craig, Derek, and I thought Ben would become paranoid and go into hiding. Ben had a lot of money because of the fraud he perpetuated with Mark. We were concerned that he'd hide "in plain sight" right here in Vietnam by paying off some of the local security apparatus: the Ministry Public Security (MPS).

The RSO office, in collaboration with DS CFI, decided that we needed to keep the information about Ben to ourselves. We knew he was connected in the community. Ben also had ties to the current consul general, a Vietnamese-American, so we kept information from him as well. Law Enforcement-Sensitive was our articulation. The CG didn't like it, and it caused some strife between the RSO office and the "Front Office"—the term used for the top government officials at any embassy or consulate. The fact that the agents from CFI investigated him made our situation even more precarious. We had a job to do; Craig explained that, direct and to the point. The Consul General might not have liked it, but it wasn't his call.

The DS CFI team came to investigate just about everyone who was associated with Mark. They reviewed his office files, interviewed his local and American staff, and also interviewed Kevin. Kevin was Mark's closest friend at the consulate. As Mark continued his illegal activity, Kevin did not know about it, so he was still hanging with Mark on a regular basis. Kevin did nothing wrong, but he was also a federal agent with another organization and in a position that had access to sensitive information. DS investigated him, and he came out clean. I considered Kevin a friend, and it was hard for me not to tell him throughout the investigation. It was even harder after Mark was arrested when Vaughn and I had to explain to him why. But Kevin understood. He knew the drill, he was in the same line of work.

The investigation by DS CFI really shit on morale at the consulate. Locals were angry and suspicious. Americans were confused because they were left in the dark about the on-goings of the investigation. DS agents were scouring the consulate talking to anybody and everybody. What little morale had already existed was gone.

Months passed before we would get word about an indictment for Ben. Scott was doing his magic behind the scenes in DC and keeping us updated as best as possible. The summer transfer season had just arrived, and both Craig and Derek were leaving. Derek was replaced with an agent named Mason. Mason was briefed on the arrest of Mark and the investigation of consulate staff. He was also briefed on the current investigation of Ben.

Shortly after Mason arrived in Ho Chi Minh City, the new RSO also arrived. Wendy was her name. Wendy had been at DS field offices for many years prior to coming overseas, but she was certainly not new to working at embassies and consulates. She had been on with DS for about fifteen years and had done her time overseas during her days as a newer agent.

Within weeks of Wendy's arrival, we got word from Scott that he finally received an arrest warrant for Ben. We were pumped, but we needed to be strategic on how to execute our plan for arrest. Ben had a lot of connections in the Vietnamese community. He could have easily paid off MPS officers and disappeared somewhere in Southeast Asia. We had to be careful not to notify the MPS too early. On the flip side, we needed their help to pinpoint his location and effect the arrest. DS agents can't make an arrest in a foreign country. We are there to facilitate, observe, and assist.

To exacerbate the situation, the U.S. does not have a MLAT agreement with Vietnam. A MLAT is a Mutual Legal Assistance Treaty which allows for "...the exchange of evidence and information in criminal related matters"[7] between the U.S. and foreign countries. It also means that because there was no MLAT

---

7 "Treaties and Agreements," https://www.state.gov/j/inl/rls/nrcrpt/2012/vol2/184110.htm.

agreement between the U.S. and Vietnam, we had to find a backdoor way to have him arrested and returned to the United States.

I presented to Wendy that I set up a meeting with our MPS contact, Colonel Vinh. Colonel Vinh was the head of the MPS Immigration Division in south Vietnam. He and I had built quite a relationship over the past two years over rice wine, Vietnamese food, and stellar karaoke singing. Colonel Vinh was a good-humored man, and I think he had a genuine like for the RSO office. Mason had not met him yet, but this was an opportunity. I didn't think it was appropriate for Wendy's first meeting with Colonel Vinh to request a favor so she stayed back at the consulate.

In the meantime Scott, back in DC, convinced the State Department Bureau of Consular Affairs to revoke Ben's passport. If his passport was revoked, technically he was in the Socialist Republic of Vietnam illegally. If he was in Vietnam as an "illegal immigrant," Colonel Vinh and his team would surely have the authority to arrest Ben and deport him. That was our way to work around the MLAT.

After a few days of waiting, Consular Affairs finally came through. They canceled Ben's passport. It was time to approach Colonel Vinh. I asked one of the RSO local staff members, Investigator Mr. Son, to contact Colonel Vinh for an important meeting. Colonel Vinh liked us so much that he decided he'd meet with as soon as possible. That meant now, at 1730 after work. As a diplomat, I'm supposed to drinking tea and eating crumpets, or in my case Pho, at this time. Nevertheless, we made our way over to see Colonel Vinh.

When we arrived to the dilapidated facility—strewn with Vietnamese flags and communist paraphernalia—we finalized or game plan. I would talk, and Mason would listen then chime in if I missed anything. This was Mason's first meeting with these officials, and since I had that rapport already built, I took the lead in explaining the details to Colonel Vinh.

Colonel Vinh did not arrive to the meeting alone. He had his staff with him: Ms. Thuy and a young male Lieutenant from the immigration division. He also brought another individual, also a Colonel but from the criminal division. I hadn't met this man before, but he seemed nice enough. He had grey hair, a big belly, and a friendly demeanor. I figured we'd have no problem. My only concern was that this new gentleman knew Ben somehow.

I started the conversation off with some light small talk.

"Colonel Vinh, very nice to see you again. I believe last time we saw each other we were at the consul general's house," I said.

Colonel Vinh responded in Vietnamese, which was translated by our investigator. "Yes, I remember that. You scored 100 on Karaoke." He turned to tell the other Colonel, "He has a very strong voice."

True. I karaoke'd my ass off the last night I saw Colonel Vinh. I sang a little John Denver "Take Me Home, Country Roads" and killed it.

But I wasn't there to talk about my songbird voice.

"Yes, Colonel, that was a great night. I think the machine was a American-made. You may remember Mr. Craig also scored 100."

"Yes, I remember. It must have been made in America. None of us Vietnamese scored 100." We all shared a laugh.

The Vietnamese take karaoke seriously. If the score says 100, you must be an outstanding singer. Not true. That machine was out of whack. I couldn't carry a tune if my life depended on it.

"Those were some good times, Colonel Minh. How is Colonel Vo? We had to take him home that night!"

Colonel Minh laughed. "Yes, he can't handle his rice wine. He is okay but has been moved to another unit."

That'll happen when you are a Colonel in a Vietnamese intelligence unit and you puke on the bathroom floor of the American Consul General's residence then get carried home by three members of the U.S. security team.

"I'm glad he's okay, Colonel."

Colonel smiled. "How can we help you Mr. Cody?"

"Well, Colonel, we have a very high-profile individual that we would like to have arrested. We think he is residing here in Ho Chi Minh City, and we were wondering if you would help us out to locate and detain him?"

Colonel Vinh smiled. "You have a U.S. arrest warrant for him?"

"Yes, sir. We do. We've also canceled his passport. It is no longer valid," I said.

"Yes, and his visa is not valid if he doesn't have a valid passport," Colonel Vinh replied.

Colonel Vinh was picking up what I was putting down, but at the moment, he wasn't the final say.

The other Colonel with grey hair spoke up. "Mr. Cody, thank you for coming to us with this issue. We have a great relationship with the United States, and we want to help you as best as possible. But we have warrants of arrest for many Vietnamese individuals in the United States, and you never send them back to us. We have sent many Americans back to the U.S. for you, but we never get that same reciprocity. When will you send us...?" He went on to name three individuals they really wanted.

This was a common discussion we had with the Vietnamese government officials. It's true. We rarely sent any Vietnamese citizens residing in the U.S. back to Vietnam on Vietnamese charges. Generally, the charges against the Vietnamese citizens residing in the United States were trumped up. For example, they wanted one individual to be sent back to Vietnam for "swindling." C'mon. If a state government in the United States had an arrest warrant for a dude charged with swindling and he was living overseas, no way we'd pay to get him back! But for the Vietnamese, it was different. The alleged swindler and all the other names they gave us were, for lack of a better term, "enemies of the state." They spoke out against Vietnamese human rights violations, privacy concerns, and illegal detainment of citizens. The Vietnamese government did not like this, for obvious reasons, so they wanted them sent back to Vietnam where they'd be thrown in jail and never seen again.

As Colonel Grey Head methodically made his argument about the U.S. never deporting Vietnamese criminals back to Vietnam, I was planning my next move. Just a week or so before, the U.S. finally, after years of negotiation, sent back one...ONE Vietnamese citizen. Well, believe me, I highlighted that one return of a Vietnamese criminal as a great success and evidence of the U.S. commitment to collaborating with Vietnam in criminal matters to the best of my ability.

"Yes, Colonel. I certainly understand your concern. We often hear this from General Minh and many of our Vietnamese government contacts. As you know, I'm not at liberty to talk about any of the individuals on that list. But what I can say is that in the past two years the relationship between the U.S. Consulate Regional Security Office and Vietnamese Government has grown exponentially. We have regular visits with each other, and when you need information from us about your family back in the U.S. or the visa processes, we are always happy to help. But, more importantly, after the many years of the U.S. not sending back any Vietnamese fugitives, just last week we finally sent one of your most wanted criminals back to you."

Colonel Grey Head said, "Yes, one. We have sent 7, 8, 9 maybe more in the last several years."

"Yes, Colonel. I understand. What I am saying is that we have built such a strong relationship with the Vietnamese government that finally we sent someone back. That has never happened before in the history of U.S relations with the Socialist Republic of Vietnam. We are making great strides, and this is a testament to how strong our relationship is between our respective offices. I have high hopes that with our continued cooperation, we will see more of this in the future." The colonel smiled and nodded. Boom, mic drop. Who's a diplomat?

The Colonel seemed pleased with my words. The truth is, however, my office relationship with MPS South had nothing to do with that Vietnamese citizen being sent back. That deal was being worked out for years before my arrival to Vietnam. True, our relationship with the Vietnamese government had grown and was much better than before. We got a lot more done than usual, but in this instance, I just used it to elevate my position on having Ben detained. As far as I was concerned, the Colonel needed to think I flew the freakin plane and delivered their fugitive personally.

"Mr. Cody, if we detain your fugitive, you will need to have him removed from the country within 24 hours," said the Colonel. "Because we are arresting him on the charge of an immigration violation, this will be an administrative charge rather than a criminal charge."

I was happy with what the Colonel was saying. However, to get Ben out of Vietnam in 24 hours would be extremely difficult. We still needed additional agents to escort him back to the U.S. and visas for those agents to get into Vietnam. That could take weeks. We also had to facilitate the logistics in the U.S. with law enforcement and tie up other loose ends.

"Thank you, Colonel. We will do our best to get him out of here within 24 hours' notice of arrest. If we are unable to and we need the time extended, is there any flexibility in the 24-hour time frame?" I asked.

"24 hours, Mr. Cody."

"Okay, Colonel. Thank you very much for your time and your support," I said. We got up, shook hands, and Colonel Vinh walked us to the front door.

I felt good about that conversation. Although the colonel didn't explicitly say he was going to detain Ben for us, he certainly indicated that was the direction he was leaning. The timeline for that, no one knew.

I headed back to the consulate to brief Wendy. "Boss, good news. They will arrest him for us. Bad news, we have to get him out 24 hours after the arrest." I explained to her why and the logistics behind it.

For the next few days, we worked with DS HQ to figure out the logistics of escorting Ben back to the U.S. We still weren't sure when Ben would be arrested. U.S. Marshals couldn't do it because they needed more than 24-hours' notice. It takes that much time just to travel there, so that would never work. DS agents from the U.S. couldn't do it because they didn't have a visa. They could make it to the Philippines or Japan, but transporting a prisoner through each of these airports is extremely difficult. The easiest path to fly out of Ho Chi Minh City was to transit through S. Korea. South Korean airlines had an excellent track record of helping us facilitate the transport of a fugitive through their airport. It also helped that Wendy was good friends with the Deputy RSO in Seoul who had excellent contacts with the police in S. Korea. So we determined what country to go through, but now who could we find to do it?

Days went by with correspondence back and forth between Wendy and DS HQ about who could transport. Because of the time 12-hour time difference, communication was slow.

The day after our meeting, Colonel Vinh's office called and said his unit was going to personally locate and detain Ben. Colonel Vinh apparently talked to the other colonel and convinced him that since Ben was being arrested on an immigration rather than criminal charge, that his unit should take the lead. Furthermore, Colonel Vinh also knew that Vietnam Interpol would be notified via a "Red Notice," or international arrest warrant. Colonel Vinh's unit, Immigration-South, did not get along with Vietnamese INTERPOL. I had met them previously; they were conceited. "Mr. Cody, Colonel Vinh said he wants to do it because you are his friend," said Mr. Son. Fuck yeah! Facebook friend's list just grew a little bit.

For reference, it is very uncommon for a Vietnamese government official to find a work-around for something of this magnitude. In the Vietnamese government structure, it is difficult for anyone to make a decision without the highest levels of the government in Hanoi approving. Some of the smallest requests often took days to approve. So the idea that Colonel Vinh just said he wanted to help us and do it before INTERPOL got wind of it was pretty much unheard of.

The phone call from Colonel Vinh came in on a Thursday afternoon. Friday came around and we hadn't heard anything until about 1600 hrs.

"Mr. Cody, Colonel Vinh called. They have Ben," said Mr. Son.

"What?! Wait, does that mean they 'have' him?"

"I don't know, sir. He just said they have him."

"OK. I need to know if he is detained because that means our clock starts now. Please go back and find out exactly what he means."

A few minutes later, Mr. Son returned and said, "They are watching him."

I knew to ask that question. Too often, when translating from one language to another, things get misinterpreted. This was one of those cases.

I walked into Wendy's office and told her they had eyes on Ben. We needed to make a decision fast but still hadn't had a solid answer from DS HQ. I told Wendy that I could escort Ben back to the U.S., but I needed someone else to go with me. Mason was down to do it. Wendy was a bit cautious because she was new to post and was concerned that with both Mason and I away that she might be overwhelmed. But then, in typical Wendy fashion, she said, "Oh hell, you guys do it. I can handle this!" and she did.

But we still waited. We couldn't do it that night. It would take us time to get tickets, coordinate further with Korean Airlines for fugitive transport, and ask South Korean Law

Enforcement to facilitate our passage through the airport. This was such short notice and on a Friday afternoon. Who works on "Federal Friday"? Everyone was going home! There was just no way to coordinate this on the weekend. After all the trouble Colonel Vinh went through behind the scenes to get approval and "take the lead" to arrest Ben, we now had to ask him if he could use his resources to watch Ben all weekend and arrest him on Monday. We asked him, a bit embarrassed about it, but he agreed.

We briefed the guys at DS HQ and they worked all weekend to coordinate with U.S. Law Enforcement contacts to take him from our custody upon arrival at Dulles. By the time we came in Monday, we just needed to coordinate the Vietnam and South Korea portion of the trip.

Monday morning rolled around, and before I was dressed, I get a phone call from Mr. Son. "Mr. Cody, Colonel Vinh's office just called me. They arrested Mr. Ben." They didn't waste any time. I threw on a suit and made my way to the office to brief Wendy. A couple hours later, we arrived at Immigration-South to see Colonel Vinh and Ben.

Upon arrival we were met by Ms. Thuy and the young lieutenant. They shook our hands, brought us inside, and offered us water. The room was set as a typical formal meeting room in Vietnam. Large wooden chairs at the head of the room sitting side-by-side with a table in the middle were overseen by a large painting of Uncle Ho, aka Ho Chi Minh, the revered "savior" of Vietnam. Along the side of each wall were multiple smaller, yet still large enough, wooden chairs that lined the walls all facing each other where staff would sit.

Agents Unknown

I took my seat under Uncle Ho and waited for Colonel Vinh's arrival. After a few minutes, he arrived with his entourage of about five people, one of which was taking pictures. I shook his hand; we exchanged greetings and made sure the camera had our good side. Colonel Vinh and I did the usual diplomatic pleasantries: so good to see you, we appreciate your hard work, our relationship is as strong as it's ever been, America and Vietnam continues to advance forward in law enforcement cooperation, so forth and so on. Then he said, "Mr. Cody, I am happy that I was able to assist you in capturing one of your most wanted fugitives. You are my friend and consider this a gift from me." As he said that, Ben was escorted in.

Ben was a small man, about 5'4" tall. Skinny with black hair, brown eyes, and of Vietnamese descent. He had long been a naturalized American citizen and was now about to face justice in the U.S.

I identified myself and Mason. "Ben, my name is Cody Perron. I'm a Special Agent with the Diplomatic Security Service. We have a federal warrant for your arrest." I showed him the warrant. "I do not intend to ask you any questions about the case, but I will read you your rights." I read his Miranda Warnings.

After I read his rights, I asked Ben if he had any questions. "What is going to happen to me?" he asked.

"We're bringing you back to the U.S. You'll remain in Vietnamese custody until we can work out the logistics. I expect you will be flying tonight or tomorrow."

"Okay, can I call anyone?"

"That's not up to me. You're in Vietnamese custody. Any other questions?" He shook his head no. "Whenever we get you on that plane, we don't plan on handcuffing you. I have flexi-cuffs if I need them, but please don't make me use them. That will be a hell of a long ride for you. Am I going to have any trouble with you?" I asked.

"No, sir."

When escorting a prisoner internationally, the airlines prefer that we do not highlight ourselves and the fugitive with handcuffs, legcuffs, or belly chains. The airlines are ultimately in control, and we must follow their rules. Law enforcement conducting fugitive transport generally assess each particular fugitive and determine how that fugitive will be restrained. This is based on a number of factors: severity of the crime, violent history, age, size, and more.

In Ben's case, we weren't too worried. There were two of us, both of which towered over him and each weighed almost a hundred pounds more than him. We had other security measures in place too. We'd stay awake the whole time; he would only get plastic utensils to eat. We had seats against the wall with no one behind us, and we sat Ben right in the middle of us.

After leaving Ben in detention with Colonel Vinh's team, we returned back to the consulate. RSO staff was already working to get us tickets on South Korean airlines. Wendy was working with the Regional Security Office in South Korea to make sure the airport police there were aware of our transit. Mason and I went home to pack. Tickets were about to be booked and our flight was scheduled for around midnight. MPS asked us to be there at 1830 to facilitate check in, search, and transport Ben.

At approximately 1800, Mason and I took a consulate vehicle to the airport and linked up with Mr. Son. We had an expedited check-in and transit through customs then went in a back room with the airport immigration police. We waited for hours, but no Ben. I'm still not sure why they wanted us to arrive so early. Finally, approximately and hour before the flight, Ben was escorted in. I reviewed his documents and showed him his one way "emergency passport" issued by the consulate. We checked his bag and conducted a body search to ensure there were no dangerous items. We were ready to go.

Shortly before boarding, Mason, Ben and I were escorted through the airport to the Korean Airline gate. We boarded before other passengers, took our seats, and prepared for the six-hour trip through the night to Seoul. I had no sleep that afternoon, and we weren't going to get sleep anytime soon.

The flight through the night was uneventful. I watched some TV, read a bit, and played an intellectually stimulating game on my iPad: Candy Crush. We arrived in Seoul around 0700 and were met by some Korean Airport Police officers who shook our hands then just allowed us to walk around their airport with our fugitive.

I was crazy hungry when I arrived in Seoul. Mason and I needed to eat, but Ben said he wasn't hungry. We bought ourselves a Burger King breakfast combo and chowed down. I bought one for Ben too just in case, but he was disinterested. Fine, more tater tots for me.

We waited in that airport for hours before our next flight. It was miserable. We were exhausted when Ben said, "I need the bathroom." I looked at Mason who was sitting across from us.

"Didn't he just take a leak?" I asked to Mason.

Then Ben said, "No, I need to do the other one."

Got it. I looked at Mason again. "He needs to deuce," I said. I wanted to be professional and play paper, rock, scissors to see who escorted him but then said, "OK, I'll go with him." We both laughed. Ben didn't.

I took Ben to the bathroom and checked out the stall to make sure there wasn't anything he could use to hurt himself. I then just stood just outside the bathroom. As men walked in and out, I kept getting this weird look as if I was trying to peek. C'mon, man.

After about ten minutes, I began to get some anxiety. I thought, "Damn, what's taking so long? Is he still in there? Did I miss him exit?" Five more minutes went by as I ruminated over these thoughts. Then…

"Oh shit, he has a belt. What if he hung himself?" I ran inside in a panic. "Ben!" I shouted. The two dudes at the urinal jumped as I yelled.

"Yes….yes, sir." His voice quivered.

"You okay in there?"

"Yes, just…just some stomach issues."

I laughed out loud. "Ok man, my bad. I'm still out here." I laughed some more—at myself, the guys that undoubtedly pissed themselves, and Ben, whose stomach issues were a direct effect of his shitty situation.

Ben emerged from the bathroom stall unscathed. I was relieved. We made our way back to Mason and, shortly thereafter, were boarding a flight to the Dulles, VA, airport.

The flight to Dulles was especially awful. It was just over twelve hours—no sleeping for the most part. Mason and I had determined that both of us staying awake was absurd. So we pulled shifts.

After Mason went to sleep, I decided to watch some movies on my iPad. I pulled up the Quentin Tarantino film "Inglourious

Basterds" and began to watch. After some time, when the "Bear Jew" decided to take off one of the Nazi's heads, I recall looking over and Ben was watching too. I thought, "Shit, this is all I need. He'll testify in court that I tried to intimidate him with this bloody movie." Not likely to happen, but after about 36 hours of no sleep, I was delirious and these thoughts played in my head. I turned off the film and began to read.

After an hour or so, Mason woke up and tapped me. It was my time to sleep. It was needed. I was nodding off throughout the flight and was certainly ineffective at that moment. I napped for a few hours and soon we were on our descent into Washington-Dulles International Airport. We woke up Ben and prepared our personal belongings.

Ben asked, "Do you know what will happen when we arrive?"

"Na man, no idea. I just know we're gonna turn you over to the U.S. Marshals at some point."

Within thirty minutes, we landed. We were all exhausted and just casually walked off the plane. Mason and I strategically stood on each side of Ben, but neither of us were holding his arm and properly escorting him. I think he was quite comfortable with us at this point. But that wouldn't last for long.

As we approached the end of the jetway, I noticed a couple plain clothes law enforcement agents with DS agent badges. It was our colleagues from the CFI office. They pointed to Ben, and two uniformed Customs and Border Protection (CBP) officers approached. They grabbed Ben just above the elbow on each arm, put him up against the wall, frisked him, and then put handcuffs on him. Ben's face turned pale. The trip with Mason and I was pleasant compared to what he would face now.

We were friendly, laughed, and joked and really did not bother him too much. But now that Ben was in full custody, the little freedoms he had were gone.

CBP whisked him away. Mason and I followed. We signed a few turnover documents, grabbed our luggage, and caught a ride from our fellow DS agents to our hotel. Shortly thereafter, we were invited up to DS HQ to meet with some higher-ups: higher-ranking DS agents. We accepted the invite and went over to the office on N. Lynn Street in Arlington, VA. Mason and I were welcomed with open arms.

"Nice work, guys. I bet you are tired." One of the bosses said as he popped open a small refrigerator and pulled out a beverage. He handed a beer to Mason and I and said "Here you go, fellas. You earned it. Anything we can do for you?"

"I'll take a bed, but first, let me kick back and enjoy this beer." We toasted to a successful fugitive return and began to tell the story of our long journey.

Chapter 7

FIRING MINH

One of the many duties of a DS special agent serving overseas is supervising security staff at U.S. Embassies or Consulates. In Ho Chi Minh City I managed the local guard force (LGF), surveillance team, investigators, administrative staff and more. I love leading people. I like being part of their lives and making their day better. I also enjoy administering change when change is necessary, developing strategies and programs to make operations more effective, and doing whatever it takes to implement a culture that everyone can buy into.

Implementing productive change in any organization is difficult. It is even more demanding and time sensitive when serving in the capacity of an Assistant Regional Security Officer (ARSO) because our time at an assignment is limited to only one to two years. By the time an ARSO sees the fruits of their labor, they could be on their way off to another assignment. Another impediment is continued resistance from local staff when trying to enact change. Often times the local employees have been in their position for over twenty years. "We've always done it this way" is generally the answer they give as they remain defiant to any type of remodeling. They feel that the programs had been established long before an ARSO's arrival, and would be around much longer after their departure. The problem is, many of the rules and policies are antiquated and ineffective. They lack ingenuity and innovation. A good ARSO will resort to new and more effective policies to keep up with the changing, technologies, trends, and threats.

I decided to pursue change in the areas that it was needed the most. The LGF was my first target. After spending some months on the ground, I could tell something wasn't right. The guard force appeared to have morale issues: they lacked motivation and were ineffective on duty. I intended to get to the bottom of it.

I started out by doing things that may appear small to some, but to the local guards, they were quite important. I made changes to the uniform. I developed a new rank structure and rank insignia. I developed uniformity in how they wear their gear. I even used some of the guards as "models" and posted the pics up in the training area and posts so that the guards knew how to carry their gear. These small changes made them beam with pride.

When they trained, I trained with them. I'd participate, coach, mentor, and generally just be around to shake hands and build a rapport. I laughed and joked with them. I learned the language and butchered it while trying to communicate with them. I tried my best to remember birthdays, be present at weddings, and congratulate them when they had a newborn. All basic stuff really.

I even created an awards program. I met with them regularly and acknowledged them in front of their peers. I could sense they were becoming more comfortable around me. I was finding the balance as their boss but also someone who genuinely cared about their welfare.

One day, I decided to attempt a strategy that I had previously tried with the surveillance team. I told the surveillance team that I wanted to hear their thoughts. I wanted to know what worked and what didn't, what problems were out there, and what solutions could work. I told them no idea was a bad idea. If the supervisor thought an idea wouldn't work, I wanted to know why it wouldn't work.

The surveillance team was made up of six surveillance detection specialists, and the plan worked like a charm. Ideas were put forth and some were adopted. We got new gear, developed new strategic plans for their operations, and overall, increased morale and effectiveness. I remember thinking, "This worked great. Let's try it with the guard force."

I soon learned that what may work for a group of six individuals does not always translate over to a larger group. The 75-person LGF dynamic was much more complex. That made sense, but the premise of my plan was the same. I wanted to hear from the people on the ground level doing the work. I laid out the same framework as I did for the surveillance team and implemented the plan.

The guard force leadership structure was as follows: the LGF Commander was the top person in charge. Under him were four shift supervisors who were responsible for guards on their shift. Another element was access guards who were in charge of their specific post. Then regular guards took up all of the other guard positions.

The first sign of trouble was when the LGF Commander, Mr. Vi, called and asked, "Anh Cody, the guards want to know if they can put their ideas in a sealed envelope and drop it into a box." I thought something must be up, and although I am a proponent of the chain of command, I had to understand why. "OK, Mr. Vi. That's fine. Make a box for them, ensure that it is sealed, and that no one tampers with it. In two weeks, I will review the items in the box."

Two weeks went by, and it was time to open up the box. I remember feeling how heavy it was. Great! A lot of ideas. Or so I thought. I did get some ideas. Some good, some just strange, but by far, the majority of the letters were complaints about one individual; a shift supervisor who they claimed was a "dictator." His name was Mr. Minh. Letter after letter stated that Mr. Minh was prejudice in his management. He was in charge of the work schedules, he signed off on incident reports, and he was the "face of the guard force" to the previous ARSO. That didn't make sense. Those are Mr. Vi's duties. I learned later that Mr. Minh literally claimed to be "untouchable."

Why did Mr. Minh feel he was untouchable? Simple. He played soccer. He was the local staff head of the consulate soccer team, and each year they had a rivalry game with the U.S. Embassy in Hanoi. The rivalry was so significant that the Consul General (CG) himself gave Mr. Minh his full support. The previous ARSOs played on the team, had beer with Mr. Minh after games, and even met with his family on the holidays. This had been going on for years. Mr. Minh had manipulated his American supervisors into thinking he was a superior leader and shift supervisor. He even attempted to have Mr. Vi fired so he could take his job.

Mr. Minh had his own group of followers in the guard force that acted as his "spies" and reported on other guards that did not fall in line with him. He had connections in the community and with the local police. Connections with police means power, in a communist country like Vietnam. Mr. Minh was even reported showing up to work drunk one day and was caught sleeping on shift. One of the guards took the picture and planned on reporting it. When Mr. Minh found out he told that guard that if he reported the incident or let that photo get out, the guard would suffer the consequences. He threatened that the police would come to that guards house and that the guard's family would pay.

I was so angry after reading these reports. Threats like this in Vietnam are real. Vietnamese who work for the U.S. consulate often suffer at the hands of local authorities. I wanted more information so I called Mr. Vi to my office.

"Mr. Vi, I have received some really disturbing reports about Mr. Minh. Have you heard about any of this?" I read him some of the reports.

"Yes, Anh Cody, I have."

"Why didn't you tell me?" I thought I had built a good enough rapport and respect with Mr. Vi that he could tell me anything.

"Anh Cody, Mr. Minh is very powerful. He played soccer with the other ARSOs. He has beers with the CG. He can get any of us fired. He threatens us!"

"He can't fire you, Mr. Vi. I won't let that happen. I want to talk to guards that are willing to come forward and discuss this with me. Some of them have listed their names. Please set these meetings up."

"Yes, Anh Cody."

"Be discreet about it. I don't want Mr. Minh learning of this and intimidating the guards. OK?"

"Surely, Anh Cody." Mr. Vi began to walk out of my office.

"And, Mr. Vi, let me tell you something. You are the guard force commander. You are their boss. I empower you to do your job; I support you in that role. If anyone ever threatens you or another guard again, I want to know about it. I don't give a damn who they know or how powerful they think they are. Is that clear?"

"Yes, Anh Cody." He turned around again to walk out.

"Oh, and Mr. Vi, fuck the CG. Security is me and Mr. Craig's show." I winked at him. He smiled and walked off.

It's true. The CG had a lot of oversight over political and economic policy that U.S. diplomats engage in. But he had very little oversight over security. The RSO empowered me to run the guard force as I saw fit. He had my back.

From the start I knew Mr. Minh was a kiss ass. I never thought he would be this detrimental to the guard force though. He'd frequently come to my office and ask me to play on the soccer team. I always denied. I had started a "boot camp" in the mornings on the consulate compound, and he'd come by after his shift and punch the heavy bag while we trained. I could see him looking to see if I was watching. After I'd leave and his five minutes of punching the bag were over, he'd leave too. He offered me to have beers with him and to meet his family. I just didn't want to, but as a leader, I also knew it wasn't right. I felt like I was undermining the power of Mr. Vi, so I never took him up on his offer.

After reading those letters, Mr. Minh's actions to befriend me became more clear. He was trying to continue his reign and maintain his status. I wasn't having it before the letters, and I certainly was not going to consider his requests now.

The information I learned after interviewing multiple guards infuriated me. One specific guard, Mr. Dung, informed me that the shift supervisors office is a "throne" to Mr. Minh. Mr. Dung described that Mr. Minh had awards, ribbons, trophies, and pictures of himself with the CG and others hung up in the office.

I asked, "Does any other supervisor have any pictures up?"

"No, sir, Anh Cody, because that is supposed to be all of their offices."

"Thank you, Mr. Dung for your candor. That will be all for now."

I called Mr. Vi immediately. "Mr. Vi, meet me at the shift supervisor's office." I stormed down to the office and took a look inside. Mr. Dung was right. Mr. Minh's paraphernalia consumed the office. Mr. Vi walked up, and I said, "Mr. Vi, this office is for all four supervisors. Not just Mr. Minh. Let's go take a look inside." We walked in together, and I pointed out items.

"See this? Take it down. This picture, take it down. This trophy, I want it out of here. Anything that has to do with Mr. Minh, unless it shows all the guards in it together, needs to be gone. I want this done within 24 hours. Is that clear?"

"Yes, Anh Cody."

"I will come to inspect. Any issues, let me know." I started to walk out.

Mr. Vi asked, "Anh Cody, what if he refuses to take it down?"

"Then put it in the trash."

A couple of days later, I noticed Mr. Minh slouching over the counter on his cell phone in the consular section, an area he wasn't supposed to be in and an area that he directed the guards not to enter. He was drinking from a water dispenser that he nor any other guards were supposed to be using: a policy he asked to have implemented because consular employees were allegedly complaining to him that the guards were in there too often. I thought, "This dude must have lost his mind!" I startled Mr. Minh as I approached.

"Mr. Minh, what are you doing?"

"Oh, hey Anh Cody! How are you?"

"I'd be better if you weren't in here but instead doing your job supervising."

"But, Anh Cody, I'm just having a break."

"I get that. There is a break room for that."

"Yes, but the other guards are in there and some are sleeping."

"Isn't there somewhere else you can take a break?"

"Yes, but I came in here to talk to my friend." Referring to his consular services friend.

I felt my temperature rise. "Let's go outside, Mr. Minh."

"Mr. Minh, didn't you ask me and Mr. Vi to implement the policy that keeps guards out of the consular section? You said consular personnel were complaining that guards are loitering in there too much?"

"Yes, Anh Cody."

"Ok..." I gave him a look. "Then why do you think it is okay for you to do it?"

"Anh Cody, he's my friend."

"Mr. Minh, what don't you understand? When I implement a policy, it applies to everyone. That includes you. Whether you had any say in the policy or not, you follow it. Do you understand?"

"Yes, Anh Cody."

"Do you know why?"

"No, Anh Cody."

"Seriously? Mr. Minh, you are their leader. You need to lead by example. If they see you do it, then they will want to do it. If they see you do it and you do not allow them to do it, that will be even worse. Does that make any sense to you?"

"Yes, Anh Cody."

"OK, now get back to work."

I took it easy on him. I was so angry. All that I had read and all the reporting I heard from others was becoming too much. But it wasn't the end.

A few weeks later, I got a call from Mr. Vi. "Anh Cody, Mr. Minh has allowed one of his friends to cut the visa line." For reference, visas to the U.S. are highly sought after. Any attempt that appears to show favoritism in any way could get an employee, Vietnamese or American, in a ton of trouble. I called Mr. Minh in my office.

"Mr. Minh, what happened earlier when you allowed someone to skip the line?"

"Oh, Anh Cody, that was just my friend. "

What is it with you and your friends? Why do you think it's ok to allow your friend to cut the line?"

"He was late." My blood was boiling.

"Mr. Minh, I don't give a damn if it was your friend or if he was late. You know you can't allow anyone to cut the line. That's against consulate policy, and it negatively impacts the RSO office and the consular section when you do that."

"But, Anh Cody, I did it before. The last ARSO allowed me to do it." He said this frequently, putting the blame on previous ARSOs.

"Mr. Minh, if I hear you bring up another ARSO again because you 'did it that way before' I'm gonna lose my shit. Those ARSOs no longer work here. You work for me now. You got that?"

"Yes, Anh Cody."

"I'll have you come by to sign a disciplinary action later in the week. Consider this your verbal counseling."

"Anh Cody! I've never had a disciplinary action! I have always got awards!"

"Mr. Minh, based on your performance, I don't know how you've ever received an award. Now get back to your post." Mr. Minh left my office looking distraught.

A couple of months went by, and Mr. Minh tried his best to keep his nose out of trouble. I could sense he felt the pressure. He was no longer his fake jovial self when I came by post. He did not like that I expected more of him as a shift supervisor. Slowly, I began to take away responsibilities from him. For example, he was no longer responsible for creating the schedule. This caused havoc on his beloved soccer team because he couldn't get all his best players off of guard duty on the weekend. After watching his dreadful performance in "leading" training, I removed that duty from him as well. He was previously in charge of managing the gas receipts for our mobile unit—a duty I thought was no longer fitting for a man with compromised integrity. I removed that duty from him too.

Those duties were then spread out to the other supervisors. This made it more fair. I could tell morale began to increase when the women and non-soccer playing guards weren't working every weekend and could spend it with their families.

The final straw came when I denied Mr. Minh's leave and he took leave anyway. He was scheduled to go on a motorbike road trip from Hanoi to Ho Chi Minh City with some of the other guards and some American staff. Some of guards already had their leave approved, but Mr. Minh waited too late to submit his leave request. If Mr. Minh was gone, this would create a shift supervisor shortage. Mr. Minh decided to take it upon himself to convince another shift supervisor into working his shift. This mean that this particular shift supervisor would work eight hours, have eight hours off, then come back on duty. When I learned that Mr. Minh had done this, I called Mr. Vi in the office.

"Mr. Vi, how is it that Mr. Minh is going on this motorbike trip? I denied his leave. He was on the schedule to work. Did you approve the schedule change?"

"Yes, Anh Cody. I did."

Generally, guards switching duty was okay as long as they had their shift covered. This is why Mr. Vi allowed it. But I was trying to make a statement that Mr. Minh can't just do whatever he wants, when he wants.

I asked Mr. Vi why he thought the guards allowed Mr. Minh to switch. "Anh Cody, truthfully, the guards like what you and Anh Craig are doing. Things are better. But they know Anh Craig will leave soon, and then you will leave after that. Mr. Minh will return to his old ways just as he did before. The guards are scared of him," he said.

I asked Mr. Vi if that was the concern of most of the guards, and he said yes. I told him he needed to tell the guards not to worry about anything. I couldn't tell Mr. Vi, but I knew that termination of Mr. Minh was just around the corner. The guy had screwed up too much. He disregarded orders, used intimidation tactics, was drunk at work, lied, and mismanaged—all of this was beginning to add up. He was a bully and I was planning on ending his reign.

I knew getting rid of Mr. Minh would be difficult, but we had to do something. One way to highlight Mr. Minh's incompetence and lack of respect for orders was to put him on a PIP: a performance improvement plan. The PIP outlines duties and tangible changes needed for an individual to be successful in the position. The PIP has a timeline associated with it and improvements must be made within this timeframe. Mr. Minh was astonished that he was put on this PIP. He felt like he didn't deserve it.

The Human Resources Manager (HRM) from the embassy in Hanoi is the person who generally handled administrative and disciplinary actions. She and I were in constant contact about Mr. Minh. I had briefed her on all the reports about him. Many of those now became official reports rather than just written on a piece of paper as a note. Guards began to stand up for themselves and take more pride in their actions. I could feel the confidence exude from some of the guards that had previously not had a voice.

Within four months my investigation into Mr. Minh's antics was coming to an end. I had continued to document all of his leadership and management failures including disciplinary actions. He was under a microscope and deservedly so. But having him removed would be no easy task. Mr. Minh had been with the consulate for over fourteen years.

After weeks of discussion, it was determined that Mr. Minh's termination from the guard force would not be possible through Human Resources. The bullying, intimidation, and down right incompetence was apparently not enough to have Mr. Minh removed. What a joke, I thought. I was so disappointed. I thought the guards that showed so much courage would continue to face Mr. Minh's wrath upon Craig's and my departure. He was going to wait us out.

I soon learned of another way to terminate Mr. Minh. Mr. Minh's lack of regard for policy and regulations and his ineptitude compromised the integrity of security at the consulate. He undermined the functionality of guards on post, and he destroyed morale. His lack of ability as a shift supervisor had been documented on many occasions. The combined information that I had was surely enough to revoke his security clearance.

I discussed with Craig, coordinated with the HRM, and confirmed this would be our strategy. The RSO did not need anyone's approval to revoke a local staff member's security clearance. The RSO office issued clearances, and we could take them away if we had evidence to prove the revocation was well-founded and justifiable.

The plan was to meet with Mr. Minh the next day, Friday, in the consulate community center (CCC). We'd have our meeting, terminate his employment, then have him escorted off the compound after giving him an opportunity to gather all of his materials.

On Friday we all met at the CCC. The community center was located just inside one of the pedestrian gates. It is a building with one large open-spaced room where the consulate would hold events. It was at the north end of the compound and right near the gate on Mac Dinh Chi Street. We set up a table with one chair on one side, a chair at the head for our translator, and two chairs on the other side for the HRM and myself. Mr. Minh spoke great English, by the way, but we wanted someone there to translate just so there could be no question as to what was being said or what was going on.

Within minutes of our arrival, Mr. Minh walked in, and I asked him to have a seat. The HRM began to speak, and she did not waste any time beating around the bush.

"Mr. Minh, today is your last day of employment at the U.S. Consulate. You are being terminated."

Mr. Minh looked at the translator incredulously, then at the HRM. "What? Why?"

"Mr. Minh, your security clearance is being pulled by the Regional Security Office. When the Regional Security Office does this, they do not have to report a reason to Human Resources. You can ask Mr. Cody after you are done signing the documents, if he chooses to share with you. I will read this official statement to you then I will need you to sign." She began to read the statement. Mr. Minh interrupted a few times, but she shut him down. She continued on as Mr. Minh sat there, shocked.

After the HRM was done reading, Mr. Minh looked at me.

"Anh Cody, but why?"

"Mr. Minh, I think you know why."

Mr. Minh said, "I have worked here for fourteen years. I have so many awards. I play soccer, and all the RSOs loved me before. I don't understand, Anh Cody. I always do my job, but you don't like me," he continued. "You never liked me. You never played soccer with me. I will call the CG and let him know what you have done."

I felt my face begin to heat up, once again. "Is this dude threatening me?" I thought. Then Mr. Minh began to insult Mr. Vi.

"I do everything for Mr. Vi; he's the reason all of this is happening." He looked at Mr. Vi, his direct supervisor, who was sitting in the room. "You did this Anh Vi! You never liked me!"

Mr. Vi stayed silent. I didn't. "Mr. Minh, that's enough," I said, but he kept trying to talk over me. "Mr. Minh, you say another word about Mr. Vi and I'll remove you from this compound myself," I said, indicating that I would physically discard him. "For months I've had guards come up to me and tell me stories of you bullying, harassing, and threatening them. For months, I've watched you fail in the performance of your duties. For months you've been fucking off when I am not looking, but when I'm around, you try to kiss my ass. I know you had a relationship with the other ARSOs, but shame on them for allowing you to blind them with your nonsense. I will not have you shit on my guards any longer. Sign these papers, and get the fuck off my compound." Mr. Minh just stared at me with a look of trepidation. He silently picked up the pen and began to sign the papers. He mumbled something in Vietnamese, but I didn't care. He was done.

After signing the documents, Mr. Minh was escorted to get his belongings by two of the guards. He went to the shift supervisor's office where he once reigned supreme with tributes to himself and pictures of his accomplishments. Nothing left remained. He was a broken man, and he brought it upon himself. Mr. Minh left his uniforms in the break room and was escorted off the compound. The news of Mr. Minh's termination spread like wildfire. Mr. Minh would no longer haunt the members of the guard force.

Mr. Minh infuriated me. He had been undermining Craig, Mr. Vi, and I for almost a year. Literally thumbing his nose at us and thinking he'd get away with it—all while telling the guards, "when they leave, I'll still be here." For weeks after Mr. Minh's departure, the myth of Mr. Minh still lingered. The guards literally thought he'd be back to work at the consulate in no time. I had to reassure them that Mr. Minh was gone and that he wielded absolutely no power. As confidence began to increase that Mr. Minh was not returning, additional guards came to tell more duplicitous stories about him. It was mind-boggling to hear all that he got away with. It was good we got rid of him.

I had an affinity for the guards. I genuinely liked them. They were hard workers, sincere, kind, and humble. Most of them realized just how good a job they had working at the consulate and would never take advantage of their position like Mr. Minh did. I hated that Mr. Minh could exploit his position like that. I despised that he did this under my watch. I was extremely saddened and disappointed when I learned of the fear in some of those men and women. And then, when the HRM said we could not do anything, I feared for them. Luckily, we had an answer.

A few weeks after Mr. Minh's termination, one of the guards who witnessed his termination saw me walking on the compound. He came over to talk to me.

"Anh Cody, thank you. The guards thank you. All of us wish we can say to Mr. Minh what you said to him. He was an awful man."

One of the female guards said, "Mr. Cody, it's like a black cloud has moved on from above us. He was so scary. We are so happy now."

Mr. Vi, an excellent guard force commander and even better person, said, "Anh Cody, you give me strength and the power to do my job. You are tough and firm yet fair, and the guards know you care about them." That meant the world to me. My intent was never to fire anyone, but to make the guard force a better operation. I think that's what I did.

Unfortunately, this was not the last time the LGF saw that I cared. In the coming weeks, something dreadful would happen. I'd be acting RSO when the the office needed leadership the most. The consulate community was about to be rocked, and we had no idea the impact it would have on our lives.

Chapter 8

A BAD DAY

The U.S. Consulate in Ho Chi Minh City, formerly known as Saigon, is one of the most historic sites in Vietnam for Americans. It was the location of the U.S. Embassy that suffered the Tet holiday bombing in 1968 and the memorable evacuation of Americans shortly before the fall of Saigon in April of 1975. Although the embassy no longer stands, a two-story building on the same beautiful grounds makes up the U.S. Consulate. With large ancient trees, a grassy knoll, and a community center where our staff gather for special events, the landscape of the property is immaculate.

The inside of the two-story consulate is made up of an open floor plan. The Consular section took up all of the bottom floor, while the second floor held the offices of the Consul General (CG), Deputy Principal Officer, Regional Security Office (RSO), Economics, Political, and other sections. My office, the RSO, was just a few doors down from the CG; the President's representative to the South of Vietnam.

I developed a special relationship with the Vietnamese staff. They are just good people. I spent time with them visiting different orphanages and even developed a "boot camp" on that grassy knoll for staff to partake in. The Vietnamese people live a much harder life than we know as Americans, but their positivity and energy are contagious.

One afternoon in September, I stood in my office jokingly arguing with one of my favorite Vietnamese staff, Linh, who was undoubtedly requesting something absurd from the security office. I forget exactly her request, but I remember explicitly denying it. "No, no. We're not doing that! Get out!" I said as I laughed and pointed to the door. She was always there to give me shit and tease me a little, an endearing quality of the Vietnamese people.

At that time I was the Acting RSO; I was in charge of security. As I was directing Linh out of my office, one of my American colleagues, Cheronda, burst through my door in a panic.

"Cody, help! Heart attack...emergency....at the warehouse!"

"Wait, what? Cheronda, calm down, tell me what's going on."

"I don't know! We need to go to the warehouse; someone is dying!"

She picked up the phone and called the motor pool to set up a ride to the warehouse. The warehouse was part of the U.S. Consulate, but it was physically located "off-site," a couple miles away. To get there quickly, we needed a ride.

"Call the medical unit and have them meet me downstairs asap," I said to the RSO Assistant. I reached in my bottom drawer and picked out the Automated External Defibrillator, or AED. Cheronda finished up her phone call, and I said "Let's go!" As we ran out of the office, I saw Mason.

"What's going on? Can I help?"

"Not sure yet. I'll call you in a bit to give you an update."

Cheronda and I made our way down the stairs and out the door to the van that was already waiting directly across from the medical unit. The nurse and doctor were still not in the van, so I ran in to get them. Nurse Mai handed me an oxygen tank and mask as she and Dr. Quyen ran to get inside the van. I was the last in, sitting just inside the sliding door behind the passenger seat.

As we left the consulate, I heard the hum of hundreds of motorbikes beeping their horns. They were all around us. Traffic was jammed—a common occurrence in Ho Chi Minh City.

When we approached our first right turn, the van had to stop for the light. In front of the light were motorbikes intending to go straight. They could have easily moved to the left to let us pass on the right. The driver honked the horn several times so that we could pass them and make a right turn. No one moved. Blasting the horn endlessly is so natural in Ho Chi Minh City no one pays any mind to it.

I was infuriated and in an obvious hurry. I quickly exited the van, ran up to the motorbikes, and politely asked them at the top of my lungs to get the fuck out of the way. They looked at me, like the mad man that I was, but they still didn't move. I began to lift the back of one motorbike with an individual still sitting on it. He looked terrified. As I did that, the light turned green, and the van began to move. I jumped into the slow-rolling van, and we made our way to the warehouse. Traffic was still heavy, but we were able to make it there in good time.

When we arrived at the warehouse, I quickly jumped up out of the van. The driver honked the horn, and the gate began to open. As the large gate slowly moved from right to left, I recall time standing still as Cheronda yelled, "Oh my god!" I took a few steps forward, turned, and looked at everyone exiting the van and said, "Everyone, get out." They didn't need to hear me say it twice. They could hear the severity of my tone and see from a distance the horrible scene: a trail of thick blood that laid in front of us, a distinct stench filled the air, and a body lay on the ground.

I walked in the gate and approached the body. It took me a second to realize who it was. The body was motionless. The face was smashed; the remaining teeth were mangled. The top of his head and forehead were shattered, and the spray of blood and brain matter covered the concrete near his body. He still had a Sprite bottle clenched in his hand. The employees that witnessed this tragedy stood there, shocked. Some had the spray of his blood on their clothes. I looked to the side of his face that was still somewhat intact and recognized the man. It was Mr. Han, a 35-year-old newly wed and one of the consulate electricians. A chill came over me.

I walked the scene in an attempt to understand what happened. I was trying to build a complete picture before I started to investigate. I remember hearing one of the guards at the scene cry out, "Mr. Cody, it was him! He did it!" Mr. Thanh was pointing at a man I didn't recognize. The man was a contractor for the consulate. He was just standing there.

"Ok, Mr. Thanh, calm down."

"It was him! I saw him!"

I still wasn't sure what exactly was going on or how Mr. Han lay there lifeless at my feet. When I looked at the contractor, he appeared remorseful and did not try to escape or run. But that didn't help. The feeling I had when Mr. Thanh yelled was extreme anger. I remember clenching my fist and looking at this contractor guy feeling that I wanted to really hurt him. Not because I think he did it purposely but because I figured he did it carelessly. That was an assumption, of course, but an assumption in that moment I felt was accurate. I have witnessed the careless behavior of individuals too many times in Vietnam. Often I would witness Vietnamese people taking shortcuts. They'd bend rules as if it were only natural. This instance appeared no different.

After taking a moment to calm down, I asked Nurse Mai and Doctor Quyen to come in. I then carefully asked all those who witnessed what happened to step away from Mr. Han's body. This was a delicate situation. My concerns were threefold: I wanted to be sensitive to those employees who witnessed this. I didn't want to contaminate the scene. And I didn't want any of the witnesses to leave. I was quite certain that this was not a crime scene, but I had to conduct a proper investigation to completely rule it out. As a federal agent, I investigate crimes. If this were an occupational accident, I would be passing this to another investigative entity. DS Headquarters would want to know exactly what happened, so I had to be diligent in my investigation.

I called Mason.

"Hey brother, can you come over and bring a crime scene kit? Bring Mr. Son and Mr. Lan with you."

"Sure thing, man. What happened?"

"A death at the warehouse. It's pretty bad."

"See you in a bit."

Mr. Son and Mr. Lan would accompany Mason to help me out. Both of these men worked for the RSO office. They were our two investigators and our right-hand men. We called on them regularly for anything relating to law enforcement.

As I waited for Mason to arrive with the crime scene kit, I asked one of the guards for a pen and paper and began to draw a schematic of the scene. I didn't know how much time I had remaining. Once the local police got wind of this, they would certainly want access to the warehouse and would try to take over. I pulled out the compass on my phone so I could be accurate on the directions on the sketch. I began to draw. I am awful at drawing.

Mason soon arrived with Mr. Son and Mr. Lan, and we got to work. Mr. Son was focused; this gruesome scene did not seem to bother him. Mr. Lan, on the other hand, struggled a bit more. I remember talking to him and noticing the blank stare on his face.

"Mr. Lan....Mr. Lan..." No response. I grabbed him by the arm. "Mr. Lan, are you OK?"

"Yes... yes sir. I think so."

"Mr. Lan, take a deep breath. It's normal for you to feel this way. I really need your help on this. Take a walk behind that truck and compose yourself; then come back and let me know if you can do it. If you can't, it's OK."

"Yes, sir."

He walked behind a big truck out of sight of the incident. He composed himself and soon made his way back over to help me. I was proud of him.

When I opened the evidence kit, I discovered it was incomplete. It had been in the RSO for many years but was never really used. It looked like previous agents may have just taken out specific items like gloves and sharpies but never replaced them. The kit should have had evidence markers, but it didn't. So we adapted and used yellow "Post-it" notes putting them next to pieces of evidence and marking the items in our makeshift evidence log. We took pictures of the evidence: long, medium, and short range. Just as we were trained. Mason and I collaborated on the sketch to make it as clear as possible. After combining our efforts to thoroughly investigate the scene, we then moved on to the arduous task of interviewing witnesses. Although many of the witnesses spoke some basic level of English, working through an interpreter is much more frustrating and therefore taxing. We worked diligently with our investigators for the next few hours interviewing witnesses.

In between one of the interviews, I recall my mouth was very dry. We had worked steadily interviewing but also breaking to answer questions from people trying to inform Mr. Han's family and the CG. I walked into one of the rooms inside the warehouse to get a glass of water when Cheronda called and told me that Mr. Han's wife wanted to come in. From a security and investigative perspective, I had no issue with his wife coming in as long as she stayed away from the evidence. We had already covered Mr. Han's body, and besides bagging the evidence, the investigation was coming to an end. From a personal perspective, I just didn't know how I felt about letting her in. I was torn. I knew she'd want to see him, and I recall just how awful Mr. Han's body was disfigured. In the end, this decision was not mine to make. I left it up to the doc, nurse, and Cheronda to make the call.

I drank my water, took a deep breath, and walked through the warehouse away from the gate. I needed some fresh air. But, just outside the gate, a large crowd had gathered to see what happened. In the crowd I saw the concerned faces of some of my colleagues and friends. Some were waving to ask me to come over. I couldn't go over, not yet. I began to get anxious. I just wanted to be away from it all for a few minutes, so I went back into the warehouse grounds and walked around the back where no one was.

Shortly after my break, I learned that the CG had arrived and wanted to come inside. While I had kept my emotions in check for the first couple hours, that was coming to an end. The CG and my office had a rocky relationship. As the security and investigations arm of the consulate, he felt we were a perpetual obstacle he had to overcome. We had previously conducted an investigation in which he was questioned, so I am certain that animosity had something to do with it.

The CG walked in and barely acknowledged Mason and me. He attempted a few comforting words to Dr. Quyen, Nurse Mai, and some of the witnesses then walked around the warehouse for a couple minutes to view the scene. Within minutes he was already calling his vehicle to leave. He had another meeting to go to that appeared to take precedence.

Prior to coming into the warehouse grounds, I informed the CG's staff to advise him that he needed to be very cautious when walking around. It seemed that message never got relayed over to him. When he decided to leave, he told the nurse and doc goodbye. Then, rather than walking around, he began to walk directly through the middle of the scene. Fortunately, I was standing nearby "protecting" it. He clumsily walked forward and almost stepped on a piece of brain. I politely checked him with my forearm knocking him off balance a bit. "Sorry, sir. You almost stepped on this piece of skull," I said. His face turned red as he became quiet and stared me in the eyes. He clearly didn't appreciate my forearm gesture.

"Cody, you need to let the local police in. They are insisting."

I had heard this request a few times already from his staffers, but I didn't really care. It was my scene.

"Sir, I get that but we're not quite finished. I'll let them in when I'm done."

"Soon Cody, they are waiting outside."

At this point the sun was going down, and I noticed a small disturbance near the gate. It looked as if someone was having a medical issue as the doctor and nurse stood over. I approached and saw Mrs. Chau, Mr. Han's new wife, lying on a stretcher. She had been allowed to view Mr. Han's body. She had an oxygen mask on her face, and her eyes were complete with shock. Seeing her panicked tears hit me hard. This was the first time I felt emotional. I felt my eyes begin to well up with tears. I was choked up on the inside too. I walked away behind the truck to compose myself.

As I returned from behind the truck, the acting Management Officer for the consulate Jerome said, "Cody, the CG says to let the police in. They are outside now and are pressuring us." At this point I had enough. The CG just told me this minutes before. He had also just barreled into my scene, showed zero sympathy, hardly asked questions, rushed out without checking in on his team, and all he can think about is allowing the cops in? Fuck that.

"I don't care if the police want to come inside nor do I give a fuck what the CG thinks. I'm waiting to hear back from the Hanoi RSO and HQ. Tell the police they can fucking wait."

"Ok, Cody. I will tell them."

I wasn't angry at Jerome, and he knew that. He was a friend. I was tired and frustrated; that anger was directed at the police and the CG.

So if you're wondering why I didn't let the police into the scene, I can just tell you that it's complicated. This was a U.S. diplomatic property on Vietnamese soil. This means that there is some level of diplomatic immunity. I say "some level" because this warehouse is an "off-site facility," meaning not on the actual consulate grounds. I was not exactly sure what particular level of immunity we could claim. On the actual consulate grounds, we had consular immunity which provides us more protections than the off-site building. I was waiting to hear back from the RSO in Hanoi and the DS HQ for further guidance.

Within the hour DS HQ got back to me. It was a friend on the other end of the line; the Deputy Director of the East Asia Pacific DS desk, Kent.

"Cody, Kent here. How you doing buddy?"

"I'm OK man. Ready to get this over with. CG is pushing me to let the local police in. What did you find out?"

"We're still working on it. Are you done doing your thing?"

"Yeah, I got all the information I needed. No crime here."

"OK then, I say let them in. But, ultimately, it's your call, when you're ready buddy."

"Roger that."

"Hey man, if you need anything else. Give me a call."

"Cool. Will do, Kent. Thanks for the support."

I hung up the phone and told Mr. Lan that he can tell the local police that they may enter.

As the local police came in and conducted their investigation, I noticed them laughing and being careless. They reminded me of a bunch of teenagers. Still, we were obligated to turn the scene over officially and let them have the evidence. I didn't need it anymore. I had determined that the incident was not a criminal act. Granted, I still had to write a report and inform HQ leadership. But there was no need for evidence. I had all the pictures I needed. This type of incident usually falls under the purview of an OSHA, or Occupational Safety and Health Association, investigation.

After relinquishing the scene, about four intense hours later, sweaty and reeking of death, I finally stepped outside to talk with Jerome and Cheronda. Both were in charge of their own consulate sections that needed to help facilitate the logistics of getting Mr. Han's body off the compound and back to his home. Both Jerome and Cheronda were also two of my closest friends at the consulate.

"You ok, Sweetie?" Cheronda asked as she gave me a big hug.

"Yeah, I'm good. So what's next?"

We discussed logistics to get Mr. Han's body back to his hometown. Both Cheronda and Jerome were already working it. A vehicle had been ordered and was on its way to pick up Mr. Han. A cleaning agency was also en route to pressure wash and clean up the mess. I was glad to have both Jerome and Cheronda there with me. All three of us were "acting" in our respective roles as Regional Security Officer, Management Officer and General Services Officer. I couldn't have asked for better teammates in those two.

After the police left, I remember walking in and seeing Nurse Mai with a mask on her face and gloves on. She was picking something up from the ground and pulling it off the walls then putting it in a bag.

"Nurse Mai, what are you doing?" Her face looked so distraught.

"Mr. Cody, I must pick up every piece of Mr. Han's body. It's very important that we return as much of his body to the family as possible," she said.

Having the body intact, or at least as much of it as possible, is important in the Buddhist religion. In order to have a proper funeral, no piece of a person's body should be left behind. The pieces she was picking up were of skull and brain matter.

The vehicle to transport Mr. Han soon came to pick him up, and some local staff escorted the body to his hometown. Once the vehicle departed, the clean-up crew came in. I walked the warehouse one last time. I noticed a gaping hole in an aluminum door and a huge dent in a steel cage just behind it. Wow, I thought, what force.

The investigation revealed that earlier during the day a company contracted by the consulate was tasked to remove a halon canister from an electrical closet. A halon canister is a type of fire extinguisher normally used to put out electrical fires. In order to effectively remove and transport it, one must follow specific guidelines. The halon canister should be strapped down during transport. The contract company did not do that. They removed the canister, put it in the back of a car, and then drove over to the consulate warehouse. Furthermore, because the canister was to be placed in the warehouse, the pressure needed be released for storage purposes. To release the pressure, one has to slowly release the valve on the copper top portion of the three-foot-tall canister. While doing this, it should be secured or else the pressure could cause the can to spin or lose control.

In this case, that is exactly what happened. The one contractor decided to release the pressure from the canister on his own. He did this too fast and lost control of it. The canister spun out of control, and the copper top smacked onto the ground. It hit the ground with such force that the neck of the canister, the most structurally vulnerable piece, broke. This sent the body of the canister flying through the air at a rapid rate of speed. It was like a missle.

At that time Mr. Han and other members of the warehouse and maintenance unit were standing in a circle talking right in front of that aluminum door, approximately fifteen feet away. The projectile flew through the air, smashed into Mr. Han's head, and then crashed through the aluminum door and stopped at a steel cage behind it. Mr. Han was killed instantly.

I made my way back to the consulate after my final walk-around. By this time it was approximately 2200. I was exhausted, both mentally and physically drained. Not so much because of what happened, although tragic, but also how and where it happened. I've seen death up close before, but this one was different. In Iraq, for example, I was mentally prepared to see death. It's part of the job in that environment. Members of our military, when sent to a combat zone, mentally prepare for it as well. Even police officers on patrol, or firemen, know that in their line of work they will see it. For me in Vietnam, one of the safest and friendly places around, doing mundane security management work on a regular basis, this was not expected. The fact I had been witness to tragic deaths before made no difference. I knew Mr. Han, I liked him. This one hurt.

Mr. Han's death took a toll on the consulate community. It was especially awful because it was a freak accident and could have been prevented. It happened to a happy, young man who was recently married and was the primary "breadwinner" of his family. We learned later that Mr. Han sent most of his money home to his family in the countryside. Having a job at the U.S. Consulate for a young Vietnamese man was a big deal. His annual salary was approximately $8,000. That's a lot of money in the Vietnamese countryside.

I sat down in my office and got to work typing up the report. Reliving all of the pictures that we took was gut-wrenching. Putting all of this on paper was even more onerous. I finished up with the report in a couple hours and sent it back to DS HQ then made my way home. I arrived home by midnight. It was a long day. Bourbon on the rocks was my drink of choice. I had a couple but still wasn't able to sleep.

The consulate community mourned Mr. Han's death the next day and for weeks to come. We held a vigil at the consulate where the CG spoke. Many of the staff, including Cheronda and I, also went to Mr. Han's home in the countryside to attend a Buddhist funeral ceremony and celebrate his life. It was moving, with pictures of Mr. Han as a little boy, pictures of his wedding, flowers, and incense. Mrs. Chau, his wife, was there. She was still the hardest for me to face.

As weeks and months passed, the community recovered. The consulate came together, and after some time mourning, Mrs. Chau was offered a part-time job at the consulate. Now, at least financially, she'd be okay. Other members of the consulate rallied together to teach her English. They gave her a lift to and from work. It was the epitome of friendship and love.

I learned that the Diplomatic Security Foundation may be able to help Mr. Han's family financially. I created a proposal and was able to articulate how Mr. Han was an asset to the RSO. He fixed lights in the Marine Security Guard Post, the air conditioner in the guard booths, and the electrical boxes that helped control some of the doors. The DS Foundation found that Mr. Han's support of the RSO was sufficient, so they donated $1,000 to Mr. Han's family.

At this time the new CG had arrived. I respected her, she was supportive of the RSO office, and an excellent leader. I wanted her to be present as I gave Mrs. Chau the check. During a small but special meeting in the CG's office I presented this check to Mrs. Chau. As I began to speak with her, I expressed my regret for her loss and my hopes for her future. I was choked up and stumbled over my words, but I think she got it. I handed her the check and asked if I could have a hug. She said yes.

Mrs. Chau and I became friends. She regularly attended consulate events. As her English got better, I was able to speak with her more frequently. She was such a good spirit. She became so good at speaking English that I could practice speaking Vietnamese with her. She helped me, but she mostly laughed at me. It was OK. I was used to it.

About nine months after the incident, I was scheduled to depart post. I asked her to meet me in the parking lot as I left work on my last day. She was accompanied by several local staff and friends. I, too, was accompanied by local staff and friends as we met in the middle of the motorbike parking lot. Mrs. Chau was a different person. She was all smiles and seemed very happy. What a difference from the first time I saw her at the warehouse.

"Good Afternoon, Mr. Cody!" she yelled. That made me smile.

"Xin Chao, Em Chau!" I responded.

I then began to tell Mrs. Chau how proud I was of her, how I respected her new accomplishments, and was inspired by her resilience. But I didn't call her out to the parking lot to give her a speech. I was there to give her something else. Mrs. Chau had been struggling with transportation, and at one point, thought that she would not be able to keep her new job at the consulate. As I finished talking, I held out a key.

"Mrs. Chau, this is the key to my motorbike. I want you to have it." Her eyes began to fill up with tears. Mine did too.

"Thank you, Mr. Cody. This makes me very happy."

With her own motorbike, and a full tank of gas, getting to work would be easy. I stole another hug.

"Hen gap lai, Em Chau."

"Goodbye, Mr. Cody."

Playing Duck, Duck, Goose at one of the local orphanages.

Agents Unknown

Ridin Dirty on my 110cc Honda Wave through the mean streets of Saigon, on our way to teach swimming lessons.

Consulate bootcamp was a hit in Ho Chi Minh City! The bootcamp took place on the beautiful consulate grounds and the historical evacuation site of American staff during the Fall of Saigon on April 30, 1975.

Chapter 9

ISIS AT THE GATES

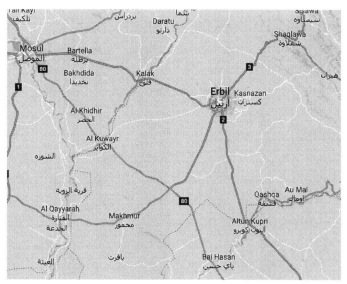

Map of the Northern Iraq and Kurdistan Region
Key Cities: Erbil, Mosul, Makhmur

I arrived in Erbil in mid-July of 2014. It was hot—the kind of hot that feels like a blow dryer hitting you in the face as you walk outside. I was met at the airport by one of the current ARSOs named Dylan. Dylan was a large man: about 6'3" tall, a robust belly, and a long goatee. He looked like a motorcycle gang member. The other portion of my security detail consisted of a local Kurdish driver and Cuba. That's the same Cuba from my Spartan 2-6 story in the Baghdad chapter. I could see Cuba's smile from inside the airport. I didn't settle for Cuba's famed fist bump but, instead, a big hug. It was good to see him again.

Dylan, Cuba, and I took the beat-up armored Chevrolet van to the consulate compound. The route from the airport was fairly simple. It was basically half a rectangle and only a few miles away from the consulate. It seemed further as transiting the airport checkpoints and entering through the consulate gates always took more time.

The consulate was set in a neighborhood of Erbil named Ankawa. Ankawa was just on the outskirts of the outer "ring" road. Erbil had several ring roads that circled the center of the city and its citadel. The U.S. government strategically chose Ankawa to set up its consulate because it was a Christian neighborhood. A Christian neighborhood, inside a predominantly Muslim country, was one of the safest locations it could be.

Being inside a Christian neighborhood certainly had its benefits. The local security apparatus, Asayish and Zervany, had checkpoints set up at all points of entry near the consulate. The Zervany "base" was nearby for a response if we needed them in an emergency. Also, the neighborhoods were small and close-knit. Christian Kurds in the neighborhood could, theoretically, notice if someone suspicious stood out. Most importantly, though, Christian Kurds drink alcohol. So do I. Getting booze in a Muslim country is no easy task. Erbil did not have a commissary as did the embassy in Baghdad. But, thanks to good ol' Christianity, whiskey and beer were in abundance on the compound.

I decided to go directly into the office as soon as I arrived to the consulate compound. The RSO office was in an Iraqi house, as were just about all the offices on compound. The office set up was a bit crammed. As I walked in the foyer area, there was a room with a couch and a desk where the Office Management Specialist, or OMS, worked. As I proceeded in further, there were two rooms to the left where the RSO and the DRSO worked. To the right was a small kitchen and a staircase leading to the rooftop. The final room was straight ahead. It was a small room with four desks crammed inside it where the ARSOs worked: the bullpen.

Upon entry I shook hands with the RSO, Ryan. I knew Ryan from many years before when he was a young ARSO in Moscow, Russia, and I was a Marine Embassy Guard. He remembered me. Prior to my arrival, we had exchanged some greetings on email. Ryan had been with DSS for approximately fifteen years or so. In his previous life, he was a teacher.

While saying hello to Ryan, the DRSO Pete came in to shake my hand. Pete was my previous colleague and supervisor from Baghdad. His unofficial call-sign was "Flanders", as in Ned Flanders from the Simpsons series. Pete had also been working with DSS for approximately fifteen years. After his tour in Baghdad, he went back to a HQ position in DC then turned right around and came back to Iraq a couple years later.

After introductions I made my way over to my house and unpacked. It was only a two-minute walk. The house was nice for third world standards. As I walked in, immediately I was standing in a kitchen. To the left was the entryway to a foyer with two bedrooms doors directly in front of me. Also to the left was a doorway to the living area with some not so comfortable government furniture already inside, and to the right a small bathroom.

These houses on the compound weren't just given to the U.S. government. We kinda took them, for a small fee of course. When the government decided it wanted to place the consulate in Ankawa, it had to make a decision: either destroy all the homes or pay the homeowners to purchase or lease their property. Since the intent was never to stay in Ankawa permanently, the government chose the latter. Some homes were purchased, and others were leased. After the buyout of homes on multiple contiguous streets, the government surrounded a the homes with T-walls. Once that was done, a few DSS approved security gates were installed and boom, you have a consulate. I suppose it wasn't as simple as my one paragraph description, but it's how I envision it went down.

The days in Erbil were long. Early wake ups for the gym, breakfast, work, lunch, maybe workout again, finish work around 1800, then be done for the night. Thank goodness for Netflix, pizza, and Bourbon.

A couple of days after my arrival, I attended a meeting at the "chancery"—another house that made up the Consul General (CG) and Deputy Consul General's office. I was there for my first meeting as the head of Protective Operations. This particular meeting was to discuss the logistics and protection of an upcoming high-level visitor. Since I was new to the Erbil position, I was there to observe and educate myself. That said, I wasn't new to DS, nor was I new to protection in high-threat environments. I was looking forward to getting my hands dirty.

Protective Ops, as it was commonly referred, was the most rewarding and exciting unit to lead. It held the most responsibility and risk but also gave me the opportunity to work with the TC guys again. Similar to the makeup of the POD in Baghdad,

Protective Ops in Erbil consisted of multiple PSD teams. These teams provided secure escort to fellow diplomats outside "the wire" to meet with their contacts. Five of the PSDs escorted regular diplomats to different venues around Erbil and across the north of Iraq. The sixth PSD was provided to the CG. The CG detail was more robust that the other five. Whereas the five regular movement teams were made up mostly of borrowed Kurdish soldiers named Zervany, the CG's team had about half TC contractors and some of the best Zervany soldiers from the whole unit.

When I walked in, I was greeted with friendly smiles from Jeff and Doug, the two TC shift leaders. I hadn't seen them since Baghdad. We hugged it out and got down to business. I was glad to be there. In the meeting I distinctly remember some of the guys saying, "We don't have enough medics, so we'll just roll without one." I remember thinking that not having a medic with a motorcade didn't feel right. But again, I was there to listen. Soon, Pete spoke up, "We need a medic on every detail with the CG and with our highest level visitors." Pete was right. The medics had to work on their day off, but it was a necessity.

After Pete left, the medic talk went on for a bit, and I remember chiming in saying, "Why don't we have medics?" The guys explained that most medics were in Baghdad. I asked, "How many do you need?" Jeff and Doug kind of chuckled. "No, I'm serious, how many medics do you need?" They explained that they could use several more medics, but based on their experience, they did not see how it would get approved. TC was short medics across the country. That did not satisfy me. I was now on a mission to get more medics.

Fortunately, I had a bit more influence this time in Iraq in my position as Chief of Protective Ops. But I also had someone who was well respected in TC and could work some angles if needed: Tony. Tony was the program manager for TC on the ground in Erbil. He and I knew each other from my time in Baghdad, both during my 60-day temporary assignment and the following year during my permanent assignment. We led low-profile teams throughout Baghdad and worked very well together. Tony, too, this time had more influence to get things done. He was well liked by the RSO office but also by TC leadership in Baghdad. Coincidently, within days of this meeting about medics, Erbil became more volatile. After some time—with the help of Tony, the increased threat in Erbil, and my perpetual bitching to the RSO and CG—we got more TC personnel, including more medics.

A few days later, we were slated to conduct a surprise compound defense drill. I hadn't even learned my way around the full compound yet, but I was ready to fill in the gaps where necessary. As the duck and cover alarms went off, everyone in the office kitted up and sprinted out the door. I thought, "That's... odd." I understood a sense of urgency in getting kitted up, but I wasn't sure why we were running out the door so fast. Once I had all my gear on, I paused for a moment then I took up a predetermined position near the office. I ended up being behind some local guards...who were behind some Americans...who were behind more Americans. It was confusing as shit. If someone came down the street, for example, and these local guards started shooting, they would be shooting over their heads or into the backs of Americans. There's one thing more to address, I thought.

After the drill—deemed a success—we had a debrief outside the office. I listened intently and kept my mouth shut. The RSO spoke, "I think everything went well." Then the DRSO gave a few words. A few TC guys made some unenthusiastic comments, and then we ended the brief. I could tell the TC guys didn't want to say anything controversial to RSO leadership, and the other agents seemed indifferent.

My concern was that as soon as the duck and cover alarm went off, people started sprinting out the doors. The duck and cover alarm is sounded by the Marine on duty. It's a "hi-low" wail, and individuals who serve at U.S. Embassies and Consulates around the world know to duck, away from windows, and take cover. In Baghdad the duck and cover sounded several times a week. Indirect fire, or IDF, was a common phenomenon and the attack of choice of IBMs. Our standard operating procedures were clear: first pause; then listen; and then, at the right time, exit…preferably after mortars are done raining down on us. So why were we sprinting out the doors in Erbil? I get it; we're security, but if we're dead because a mortar landed on our head, we are useless.

After the brief I brought it up to Dylan who sympathized with my concerns. I then brought it up to the TC guys and asked them if they saw any issues running out immediately. The senior TC contractors who had been around a while looked defeated as I asked the question. They had been wondering this for a long time, and it was clear they disagreed with the policy. I then asked Tony, "Tony, something's off. How long have y'all just been running outside when y'all hear the duck and cover?" He responded, "Too long, Cody, too long. We brought it up before, but the RSO believes this is the best policy." It was apparent that Tony didn't agree with this policy either. Tony was stuck in a hard place. He couldn't overtly ridicule the policy of the RSO to his "troops," but he certainly didn't agree with it. He also couldn't continue to badger the RSO about it or his position could be in jeopardy. It was a battle Tony was no longer willing to fight. But I was.

I went into the RSO's office to speak to him privately.

"Sir, can I talk to you?"

"Sure, Cody. What's up?" he asked.

"Sir, I have some concerns about the compound defense plan. I don't think it's the best idea to run outside immediately when the duck and cover sounds. We should pause for a few seconds, maybe even minutes, to make sure it's not IDF."

He responded, "Yeah, I guess, Cody. I've heard that before. It's just, we haven't ever had IDF here in Erbil, so it's best that the guys just get out to their positions as soon as possible."

"Yes, sir. I see the need to get out to positions, but a few seconds won't cause a major issue, particularly if by pausing, we could save some lives." I could see the frustration on his face.

"We'll just keep this policy, Cody," he said.

I wanted to say something, but I was too new. "Roger that, sir," I said. This battle wasn't over though.

A few weeks later, around mid-August, I was sound asleep around 0200 when I got a call from my contact from the off-site National Intelligence Operations Compound (NIOC) in Erbil. Since one of the duties of my position was to be the State Department security liaison to the NIOC, all calls from that compound came to me.

As I woke up from my slumber to hear the voice of my intelligence contact, I felt his sense of urgency.

"Cody, I need you to check your red-side email." Red-side, or high-side, email means my classified email account.

"Bro, it's 0200. Can't it wait?" I asked—as any lazy public servant would.

"No, you need to see this asap," he said.

"Shit, OK, I will head that way now."

At this point ISIS has been in Iraq for a while. They had fully consumed Mosul, were on the outskirts of Baghdad, and on the border the Kurdistan region, where Erbil is located. During my security brief prior to coming to Erbil, the analyst said that ISIS didn't want anything to do with Kurdistan. He was wrong. ISIS wanted their piece of the northern Iraq region as well.

I got dressed and made my way over to our TOC. On my way I saw the bosses Ryan and Pete.

"Hey, Cody, have you been up to the rooftops yet?" Ryan asked.

"No, sir. It's 0200."

"Oh, well, you should go check it out."

"Roger that, sir. Gotta check the high-side first. NIOC sent me something."

"Just go up and take a look before you check your high side," Ryan said.

So I walked up the street, past the gym, and to the northwest side of the compound where a local guard was posted at the top of an observation tower. When I reached the top, what I saw was disturbing. The gas station to the north was lined with cars as far as I could see. The gas station in the distance to the southwest was packed as well. There was a traffic jam on the ring road all headed in the same direction out of town. It was a sea of red tail lights.

I left the guard post and made my way over to the TOC to check my high-side email. The email I received was also alarming. The specificity of the information in the email is sensitive so I cannot share it. I'll just say this: there were a lot of ISIS fighters headed our way. ISIS had just taken the last city before reaching Erbil, and we were outnumbered by the hundreds.

As I came out of the TOC, I saw Ryan and Pete again in the street.

"Sir, I just forwarded you an email. You need to see it asap," I said.

"OK, Cody. I'll get to it in a bit."

"Roger that, sir. Just so you know, it's regarding all the chaos going on outside the gates."

As I walked off, I called Tony. He answered pretty quick.

"Yo man, you see what's going on outside the gates?"

"Yeah, the guys called me earlier to tell me," he said.

"Cool. Let's meet. I need to share some intel."

I met with Tony and briefed him on the intelligence I had received. We decided on setting up observation posts. At this time we had less than fifty "shooters" on the compound, made up of TC, Marines, and six DS agents. I didn't want to rattle anyone, so I asked Tony that he discreetly get a team prepared to take up posts on the rooftop. In fifteen minutes or so, Tony called, "All good, Cody. The guys are up, and I set up a rotation."

After talking with Tony, I found Ryan again.

"Sir, have you been in contact with the MEU?"

"About six weeks back I executed a plan with them, but I haven't heard back. Then again, I don't check my high-side so often," Ryan kind of chuckled.

Shit. They could have been in touch, and we wouldn't know. "We need to get in contact with them. Do you have their info, and do you mind if I contact them?" I asked.

"I do have it, and actually, that'd be great! I'll send you all of the emails they've sent me, and you can reach out to them and coordinate."

"Sounds good, sir."

Upon receiving Ryan's forwards, I called up the Commanding Officer (CO) of the FAST on the MEU. MEU stands for Marine Expeditionary Unit. It is a forward-deployed, expeditionary quick reaction force that is prepared for immediate response whether combat, contingency operations, natural disasters, or any other assignment directed by the Secretary of Defense. [8] FAST stands for Fleet Antiterrorism Security Team. They were the component of the MEU that would, theoretically, come rescue us if shit went down hill.

The phone ringed a few times, and then there was an answer. I asked for Captain Smith, and shortly after, I was connected.

"Captain Smith here."

"Captain, Cody Perron. I'm with the Regional Security Office in Erbil. My boss tells me you executed a plan weeks back?" I asked.

"Yes, sir! I've been waiting to hear from you guys. We have a plan, but we just want to know the status on the ground now." I was surprised when he said he was waiting to hear from us. Then again, our classified communications were all jacked up.

I briefed Captain Smith.

---
[8] "Amphibious Ready Group And Marine Expeditionary Unit Overview," http://www.marines.mil/Portals/59/Amphibious%20Ready%20Group%20And%20Marine%20Expeditionary%20Unit%20Overview.pdf.

"What's your current location?" I asked.

"In the Persian Gulf, but we have a platoon stationed in Baghdad at the moment. I could backfill them and get a platoon to you if needed."

Baghdad needed them; ISIS was still aggressively pushing towards the capital city and was gaining ground.

"Roger that, Captain. I'll pass this info to the boss. He and the CG would need to approve of that, but I like the idea. If you need me in the meantime, call me back on my cell, and I'll find a secure line to call you back on."

"Sounds good, Cody. Out."

At least we had contact now. A step in the right direction.

I headed back to the office to brief Ryan. As I returned, I noticed that Pete and another agent, Aaron, were in the office putting in time. The word was spreading fast. I sat in my desk and began to reply to some emails.

Shortly thereafter, Todd, one of my protective ops guys, arrived at the office with all his tactical gear and weapons. He was wearing a "flight suit with a drop holster."

"Dude, what's up?" I asked him.

"I heard we might have to fight," he said.

I chuckled a bit. "Not yet bud, but you look like you're prepared."

"Yep!" he said.

Todd was perpetually prepared.

Soon Tony walked in, laughing. French Montana's song "Ain't Worried 'Bout Nothing" was playing.

"What's going on, Cody?" he asked.

"Oh, you know. Ready to fuck shit up. Or get overrun. Whatevs."

We all had a good, yet nervous chuckle.

After chatting with Tony a bit and tossing ideas about security items we needed to update in order to hold the compound, I retired to my room to get a couple hours of sleep. We all needed to get some sleep. ISIS was still twenty miles away or so, and they had to get through the Kurdish front lines. Plus, this could be the last time we got sleep for a while.

The next day, I started early. Everyone was in the office by 0600. Pete called me in and asked that I oversee preparations for compound defense and possible evacuation. Leaving the compound in a hurry and under pressure would be no small task. We had hundreds of people we had to move, and if we weren't able to move them, we'd have to hunker down and defend ourselves.

I stepped away and began to execute a plan in my head. I called Tony over, and we consulted each other. I knew that if were going to do this efficiently, I needed the full support from Pete. So I went in to ask him for his approval on several items.

"Boss, I think our DDMs (Designated Defensive Marksman aka Snipers) should keep their weapons in their room. I also think the 240s (machine guns) should be on the observations posts or with shooters in their room. We won't have time to pull them from the armory if an attack is imminent."

Pete saw my sense of urgency and said, "Sure, Cody, do what you need to do. Just send me an email for documentation purposes of what exactly you're doing, and I will approve. The TC guys will want some top cover."

"Roger that, boss." I liked Pete's style.

One of the first things we needed to do was destroy classified material and sensitive documents. So we got barrels, dumped files inside, filled them with gas, and started burning. Items that couldn't be burned were smashed with sledgehammers. The guys in the TOC began using armored vehicles to run over and smash the harder items. All of it was fair game. We just had to destroy it and destroy it fast.

As the destruction process was going on, we also needed to beef up our internal security, and we had to do it quickly. Sure, we had security plans already, but we needed to augment positions as best as possible with every asset we had. I started by walking with a team of guys to identify and then set up new observation posts and blocking positions. We also immediately changed the duck and cover policy from the "running outside as soon as we heard the alarm" to pausing, listening, and then taking up positions. This policy change was a win. Several months later, a rocket did reach Erbil, landing right near the airport.

Preparing for an evacuation was also necessary. I had the team members start up the vehicles and drive them around the compound. They ensured the gas tanks were full and that the tires were inflated. Inside the vehicles were extra PPE and medical kits. We implemented a hasty plan to motorcade out of there while protecting our colleagues. It was going to be one hell of a long motorcade if we had to execute.

Lastly, we needed to work on getting all the support we could, particularly all available USG assets. I called my security contact at the NIOC and asked him to come over to conduct some tactical planning. When I got in touch with Jeremy, he was ready and willing to come over and work together. As a former Recon Marine, Jeremy understood that we were short on weapons and manpower, and if the shit went down hill, we'd need help. Together we collaborated and developed a plan: communication protocol, evacuation routes, personnel and staffing, and logistics. You name it; we did it. Jeremy and I worked on this for hours. Granted, it was a "hasty" plan. It was completed quick and in a hurry, but we were confident it would be effective. Before Jeremy left I gave him one of our PRC-152 tactical radios to bring back to his command post so that we could conduct regular radio checks with our TOC. This situation seemed all too familiar to the reports we read on the attack at the consulate in Benghazi. We weren't going to allow that to happen. We were prepared.

When I came out of my planning meeting with Jeremy, one of the TC shift leaders approached me. "Sir, we have a lot of questions about what our limitations are."

"Shoot," I said.

The conversation went something like this: Can we use the M203 grenade launchers? Yup. Can we strategically pre place ammo? Do it. Can we fill up Suburbans with the optics so that if we need to destroy them in a hurry we'll just run over them? Sounds like a plan. But the best was…

"Sir, can we carry thermite?" One guy asked.

"Wait, what? Why?"

"So we can blow up the remaining Suburbans as we leave."

I laughed. "I don't think we're gonna be walking off the commpound with vehicles blowing up in the background like Denzel, but it's good to be prepared. We'll keep them in strategic locations and locked up. No one should personally keep any thermite," I said.

"Roger that, sir."

"Bro," I reiterated, "No one should have any thermite on their person."

He laughed, "Yes, sir."

The day went on as we continued preparations, and soon the sun would be setting. Men were rotating on post. I went up to visit with them for a few hours, brought some food, and talked some shit. They were in good spirits. Ready to fight if necessary.

Around 0100 I retired to bed to try and get some shut-eye. I slept fully clothed, with my radio on, rifle in my bed, kit on the floor, and phone next to my head. It was difficult to sleep knowing that ISIS was at the gates of Kurdistan, only about twenty five miles away to the south, terrorizing the town of Makhmur and thirty five miles to the west still wreaking havoc on the city of Mosul. They were moving at a rapid pace towards Erbil with the U.S. consulate in their crosshairs. I watched the news in my room before closing my eyes, and I didn't see any reporting on our current situation. Maybe I was on the wrong channel. I wondered if anyone in America knew, or if anyone cared, as I drifted to sleep.

The next day, I woke up around 0600 again. I was surprised that I wasn't awakened in the middle of the night. I walked to the door in my living area and opened it. It was eerily quiet: no sounds of cars passing by, no motorbikes, and no horns. It seemed the city had completely evacuated. Then, as I listened carefully, I could hear something in the distance: *boom*. I heard it once, then again, and again. Something was up.

I went into the office to check it out. I learned that ISIS pushed passed the city of Makhmur, advancing five miles closer to Erbil: only twenty miles away now. But they got too close.

Agents Unknown

I turned on the news and learned that President Obama authorized limited airstrikes[9] on the ISIS advance towards Erbil, thwarting their attempt to capture the capital of Kurdistan and, ultimately, the U.S. consulate. Reports indicated that the ISIS fighters were fleeing and going in the opposite direction. A sense of relief came over me. I poured myself a cup of coffee, sat back at my desk, started reading emails, and turned on some music. No fight today. We were going to be around a bit longer. America!

Hangin with Flat Stanley outside Domiz Refugee Camp in Duhok, Iraq.

---

9 Cooper, Landler, and Rubin, "Obama Allows Limited Airstrikes on ISIS," *New York Times*, (August 2014). https://www.nytimes.com/2014/08/08/world/middleeast/obama-weighs-military-strikes-to-aid-trapped-iraqis-officials-say.html.

I met this young man at a camp near the Syrian Border. He wears the picture of his mom on his chest. She was killed by ISIS. When asked what he wants to be when he grows up. "I want to be a soldier."

Agents Unknown

This was on a protection mission towards the city of Makhmur, at the Kurdish front lines in the fight with ISIS.

Chapter 10

BECAUSE OF DELAL

Kayla Mueller, a 26-year-old aid worker from Arizona went missing in 2013. She crossed into Syria from Turkey, accompanying a friend who worked for Doctors Without Borders. That was the last anyone heard from her. Since Kayla vanished, the U.S. government had no leads regarding her whereabouts. This was the first one. The young Yezidi girl was held captive with Kayla and could provide, thus far, the only information regarding her imprisonment and disappearance.

As we whipped around the streets of Duhok, the magnitude of what was about to happen was gripping me. I was nervous. I'm a special agent, a criminal investigator. I'm not trained to conduct former hostage interviews, especially of a child or adolescent. But I am a human—a brother to a sister and an uncle to five nieces. I needed to find the balance between professionalism and compassion. This could be the most important interview of my career and could lead to a successful recovery of an American.

As the taxi made its final turn, we were dropped off at the edge of a driveway to what appeared to be a shopping center. I remember walking uphill past the shopping center to the United Nations High Commission for Refugees (UNHCR). As I looked around at this surreal northern Iraqi city, I remember seeing a ferris wheel and saying, "Ali, what the fuck is a ferris wheel doing in the middle of shopping center?" Ali laughed. And I thought there was no fun in Iraq.

I called our point of contact at the UNHCR who directed us to the entrance. As we approached, an elderly man, who looked to be in his sixties, and a young blonde lady, probably in her early thirties, greeted us. They shook our hands, took us inside, and sat us down in a small room. They offered us some water and asked us if the blonde lady could join us in the interview. They felt it would make the girls more comfortable. Sure. I was on their turf, so no problem. I wanted them to feel safe.

Within minutes, the man returned with the two young ladies. Both of them appeared exhausted. One, Delal, was tall with light blue eyes, fair skin, and light-brown hair. She had a distinct look, with a pointy nose and sharp features common of ethnic Yezidis. The other girl, Souza, was a bit shorter. She was chunky, like sweet and innocent chunky, with black hair and dark-brown eyes. They were both fifteen years old. It was clear upon their entrance, and throughout the interview, that Delal was the leader.

I started the interview by introducing myself with Ali interpreting. I began by telling her why I was there and that at anytime if she did not feel comfortable or needed a break, to let me know. She agreed and we continued. I then asked Delal basic questions: name, date of birth, place of birth, parents names, etc. These were normal biographical questions that are asked in most investigative interviews. Then I asked her to tell her story. I remembered in training that I wanted to ask "open-ended" questions. I just wanted her to talk, to tell me her version of events, and then as we progressed, if something wasn't clear, I would ask for more specificity.

Delal began to tell me about her tragic experience. In early September 2014, ISIS began to raid their village. Delal and her family members hurried to leave the city. Her father, mother, and sister all fled on foot with very few personal items. Delal stated that after some time, not long after they started running, they were captured. ISIS had vehicles, and they were moving at a rapid pace. Delal stated that once they were captured, the males were separated from the females. Her dad and mom, she explained, were ripped off the bus and shortly thereafter executed on their knees. Delal was then separated from her sister. When asked why she thought she was separated, Delal stated, "…because she was ugly. ISIS separated the pretty girls from the ugly girls because they could get more money selling the pretty girls." She never saw her sister again.

In the coming weeks, Delal was taken to several different towns blindfolded. She was sold to at least four different men, in four different towns—all of which raped and abused her. She told me that she tried to escape two other times, but both attempts failed. After her second attempt, she was caught, brought back to a prison cell, and chained to the floor. Because she was the leader of the escape, the ISIS guards made her watch as her friend was brutally raped then stoned to death in front of her. Delal broke her arm in that incident as she struggled, twisting and turning, in an attempt to free herself and help her friend.

The last person Delal was sold to was an individual she described as a fat man with a reddish beard and thick black hair. She told me it seemed that he was rich because there were guards around his home, whereas the other men she was previously sold to had no guards. She further stated that the man had two other girls there: Souza and Kayla. He also had a wife who she stated was very mean to her. The wife verbally and physically abused Delal. The fat man raped the girls a few times a week, but Kayla was his favorite. When asked why Kayla was his favorite, she said "Because she's American."

I then pulled out my folder which had some pictures in it I pulled off of the internet of Kayla.

I asked Delal, "Would you be willing to look at some pictures for me?"

"Yes," she said.

"If I show you a picture of a girl, would you be able to identify if it is Kayla?"

"Yes," she replied. "I think so."

I pulled out the first photo.

"Yes."

Then a second.

"Yes."

Then another.

She began to tear up. "Yes."

"Okay, Delal. That's it. I won't show any more photos." I handed her a tissue and asked her if she needed a break.

"No. I'm okay," she said.

I asked Delal to give me a description of the house. She had some detailed information about the layout because she was often moved from room to room. She told me about the different areas in the large house: the kitchen, bathrooms, three bedrooms, and the staircase. The girls were never allowed upstairs. I asked Delal to describe entry and exits, the size of the doors, which way did they open, and what they were made of. I asked what type of locks were on the doors, if any security devices were present on them, and if they were always locked. I drew what I thought was a schematic of the house, eventually to turn over to the special operations to see if they could use it.

I then began to ask questions about the times she was moved from the house. She stated that several times a week, the girls were transported from the main home to another then back again. I knew she was blindfolded, but I asked her if she remembered sensing anything. She told me that she remembered smelling gas. She also said sometimes she could see under her blindfold and noticed big machines in the field at a distance. I determined from her descriptions that she was looking at oil drills. I asked what time of day she was usually transported, and she said in the morning. So then I asked if she remembers where the sun was in relation to her when she was being moved. She stated in front of her. She remembers it vividly because it felt good on her face. Traveling towards the sun in the morning equals traveling east. She returned in the evening, and the sun was in her face again. Boom. I solved it. East in the morning, west in the evening. She's in...shit. I don't know, does this even help? I figured I'd pass it to the special operations guys, and maybe they could triangulate it or make something out of it.

After my initial line of questioning, the Army analyst had his shot. The analyst asked his questions and got many of the responses he was looking for. In particular he showed some photos of individuals the special operations team had their eye on: some High Value Targets. I believe he showed approximately ten photos of different dickheads; she recognized two of them. One of them she noticed was a security guard at one of the locations she was held, possibly in Al-Raqqah.

After the analyst's questioning, we went over the details of her escape. Delal and Souza escaped late one night, approximately two weeks prior, so likely around early October. When I asked her what would have happened to her if she was caught escaping this time, she said they would have killed her. So then I asked her, "Why risk it? Why try to escape again?" She said, "I'd rather die than live like this." Fuck, Cody, stupid question.

Delal said she and Souza escaped through a small window that was laced with barbed wire. But as the girls exited the window, they realized that they did not have their head scarves. Delal went back through the barbed wire window and retrieved it while Souza crouched down out of sight.

I asked, "Where was Kayla during your escape?"

"Asleep in the bed."

"In the same room? Didn't she wake up?"

"No. She was so tired and didn't want to be a part of it," Delal said. When I asked Delal why, she said, "Kayla had given up. She was tired and lost hope."

As Delal went back into that window the second time, Delal kissed Kayla her on the eyes and proceeded through the window again. That would be the last time she ever saw her.

As the girls proceeded out of the window into a walled backyard, they noticed something pushed against the wall. She decided that they could use whatever it was to propel themselves over. So they did. As they hit the ground, they saw one of the ISIS guards to their left. To their right they heard a dog barking. They decided to proceed straight into the wooded area.

After a few hours hiding out in the forest, the girls were getting concerned. The sun would soon rise, and they could be discovered. They needed to act fast.

Delal surveyed the area and noticed a home with all of the lights on. She wanted to go knock on the door. Souza was scared and begged Delal not to do it, but Delal didn't care. She had to take this chance. Delal chose this particular home because it was the only house with a light on. All the other homes in the town turned the lights out at night to avoid air strikes. This one didn't. Delal knew going to knock on the door of this house was going to be a major risk, but she couldn't escape the area without someone's help.

Delal knocked on the door, and Souza stood behind her. The door opened and a man opened. Delal explained their situation to the man at the door, and he allowed them to come in. He was alone in the house and initially treated the girls well. He said that he would do everything that he could to get them to safety. But suddenly, within minutes, Delal said he became aggressive. He saw an opportunity to make a profit and began to threaten the girls. He told them that he would sell them back to ISIS if they didn't give him some money.

Delal was allowed to call her cousin. She was able to get in touch with him, and after some time, the cousin returned the call and said he could provide the equivalent of seven thousand U.S. dollars. That's a lot of money in Syria. The man agreed to the price, so they prepared for the trip out of the ISIS-controlled territory. As darkness fell later that night the man put the girls on the back of his motorbike, cover them with a blanket, and drive out of the town of Deir ez-Zur. The three drove on a motorbike for seventeen hours ending their journey in Al Ashakah, a Syrian town near the Iraqi border.

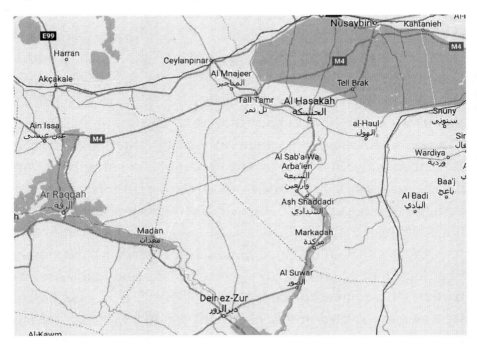

After a long journey of avoiding ISIS militants, they finally arrived and Delal saw her cousin. She ran into his arms, they embraced and collapsed to the ground. Souza joined in as well.

The girls had been through inconceivable torture. They experienced the brutality of savages. Delal witnessed the execution of her parents and the rape and death of her friends. She was sold for sex in a cage and chained to a floor. Throughout all of this, she never gave up hope. She never quit. She displayed a resilience I have never witnessed from any human before.

When the interview was over, I took a taxi back to the base, got on the helicopter, and made my way back to Erbil to write my report. I wanted to get this information to the right sources as soon as possible. I arrived back to the safety of the U.S. Consulate compound in the early evening. Some of my team members picked me up, and I distinctly remember one asking me, "How'd it go, sir?" I remember getting goosebumps "Good. It was good" I said as I laid my head back on the head rest.

Two days after to returning to Erbil, it was my turn to go on leave. Three weeks of freedom were ahead of me, and I was going to Southeast Asia to visit with friends in the region. But I couldn't stop thinking about Delal and what would happen to her. I wanted so much to help, but there was nothing more I could do. The special operations guys would take over from here, and I had hopes that they'd help her out and find Kayla.

After my three weeks of leave, I returned back to Erbil and called my contact at the special operations. The guys I normally dealt with had rotated out. The new guy was a Sergeant Major in the Army. He was a member of the U.S. Army's elite Delta Force, also known as CAG, or the Unit. I hadn't met him yet, but my previous special operations contacts had briefed me about him and gave me his contact info. I was surprised to learn that he also heard of me and read my report.

Since my first report that October day, the special operations guys had been back to meet Delal in Duhok approximately ten times. They decided they were going to bring her to Erbil to get all of the information they could for a potential future operation. At the time he couldn't tell me much more. I remember him saying, "Cody, when this op goes down, and it's all over with, I'll buy you a beer and tell you all about it. Probably before Christmas." That's all I wanted to hear.

An operation did go down, but it was not by Christmas time. It was many months later around June and shortly before the end of my tour in Erbil. I was on my final batch of leave days and I remember hearing something in the news about a raid by U.S. Special Operations in Syria. I listened intently. They raided the home of the ISIS "emir of oil and gas" in the town of Deir ez-Zour.[10] His name was Abu Sayyaf. I had a strong feeling this was the guy that was holding Kayla and the home that Delal had escaped from. The raid yielded what was described as a "treasure trove of material."[11]

When I returned to Erbil I contacted the special operations Sergeant Major to schedule a meeting. The special operations guys were coming to the consulate compound to pick up some of the ancient artifacts they also recovered in the raid on Abu Sayyaf's home. These were artifacts from the now-destroyed Mosul Museum: some of the oldest and most historical items dating back to the seventh century B.C.[12] The items were being held in our TOC.

This next time when I spoke to the Sergeant Major he told me something similar to what I heard in the news: the operation yielded terabytes of information on ISIS financing and future terrorist attacks. Furthermore, they recovered all of these antiquities. But, unfortunately, Kayla was no longer there.

It was confirmed that the house they raided was the house I described in my report: the house where Kayla, Delal, and Souza

---

10 E. Schmitt, "Commando Raids on ISIS Yield Vital Data in Shadowy War," *New York Times*, (June 2017). https://www.nytimes.com/2017/06/25/world/middleeast/islamic-state-syria-raqqa-special-operations.html.

11 Cooper, Landler, and Rubin, "Obama Allows Limited Airstrikes on ISIS," *New York Times*, (August 2014). https://www.nytimes.com/2014/08/08/world/middleeast/obama-weighs-military-strikes-to-aid-trapped-iraqis-officials-say.html.

12 Ben Wedeman, "ISIS devastated Mosul Museum, or did it?," *CNN*, (December 2017). http://www.cnn.com/2017/03/12/middleeast/mosul-museum-isis/index.html.

were held captive. They further confirmed that they killed Abu Sayyaf and captured Umm Sayyaf, his wife. They also rescued another Yezidi hostage. That's a win but not the end of the game. Kayla was still out there, and they were going to find her. Or so I thought.

The special operations worked day and night trying to pinpoint Kayla's whereabouts. If they found her location, they would have undoubtedly done their best to rescue her, pending approval from the desks in Washington, D.C.

Unfortunately, I left Erbil before any other attempts to arrest Kayla. I was at my new assignment in San Diego when I saw on the news that Kayla was allegedly killed in a Jordanian airstrike. Whether the actual airstrike was her cause of death or not, it was apparent that she was deceased.

As for Delal and Souza, I am unsure what exactly happened to them. The last I heard, the U.S. government was working to get them a visa to America with approximately ten of their family members. They were supposed to get some help from a Refugee Assistance Program that the USG offers and also receive a sizeable amount of award money.

Every once in a while, I see news stories about two girls who were held hostage with Kayla. Their images are usually blacked out and distorted. The BBC reported a strikingly similar story with both Delal and Souza's names, spelled Dalal and Susan. I feel confident this is the same Delal that I interviewed only weeks after her escape from ISIS.

I later learned through news sources that Abu Bakr Al Baghdadi, the ISIS leader, was allegedly using Abu Sayyaf's home to rape Kayla.[13] I don't know how much of this is true, but I did briefly recall a conversation I had with one of the special operations team members who also indicated this was a strong possibility.

This interview, and the other work I conducted in Erbil, was the pinnacle of my career with the DSS. I don't think I will ever serve in a position with so much responsibility that is so rewarding. We did some good work in Erbil, and in this case, with special operations in the lead: A high-level terrorist was killed, potential terrorist attacks were thwarted, and another girl rescued. Score one for the good guys.

---

13 "US hostage Kayla Mueller 'killed by IS', say ex-slaves," http://www.bbc.com/news/world-middle-east-34205911.

Chapter 11

YOU DON'T WANT THIS

Serving in a high-threat environment like Iraq can bring out both the best and worst in people. As each individual struggles with being away from home and family, locked down with danger perpetually lingering, they tend to become an alternate version of themselves. I saw this during both of my tours with the State Department in Iraq. I witnessed mental breakdowns, alcoholism, and suicides, unfortunately, on numerous occasions. And although it's possible that there could be underlying factors before an individual comes to post, being at these posts can exacerbate any internal crisis one is dealing with. I came face to face with this issue early one morning while in Erbil.

"Sir, Colonel Lewis is flipping out. He crawled over the rooftops from his office to the weight room. He is punching the wall and won't stop yelling," the shift leader from our emergency response (ERT) team said.

"What? He crawled over the rooftops? That's like four buildings over" I said.

"Yes, I think he's drunk."

"OK, I'll be there in a few."

I dressed and made my way over to the ERT office on the other side of the consulate compound.

Colonel Lewis was a U.S. Army Colonel who was working in Erbil as the pointman for the Office of Security Cooperation-Iraq, or OSC-I. He was a super nice guy, and although he often pushed the limits of RSO rules, he was still a friend of the office. Because he was assigned to OSC-I, it means that he fell under Chief of Mission (COM) authority rather than under the military combatant command authority. What this means is that although he reported to his military superiors in Baghdad, he also reported to the Ambassador, who is a civilian and the COM. In Erbil, he reported directly to the CG, the Ambassadors representative in the North of Iraq. Furthermore, because he was under COM authority, he fell under the rules of the Regional Security Office.

Earlier that evening, a friend of the CG and one of the consulates primary contacts had a relative getting married in the city. The request came to the RSO office for approval to allow twelve individuals to attend this wedding and the subsequent after party. For reference, no one in Erbil is allowed to leave the consulate compound without a PSD. Also, the general rule is that individuals are not allowed to drink off-compound because they would be returning with a PSD. The PSD agent in charge needs everyone to be coherent so that, in the event of a security incident, they can react accordingly and help themselves. On occasion, that rule was overlooked so diplomats could have a drink or two with their contacts, as long as the amount of alcohol intake was reasonable. Being completely intoxicated is never allowed. Who dictates what is reasonable? No one really.

On this particular evening, we knew this would be an issue, we addressed it and advised that although drinking will be allowed, everyone needed to drink responsibly; whatever that means.

Within minutes, I arrived at the ERT office. I walked up the stairs to the rooftop where there was a small external room that housed a weight bench, a few weights, kettlebells, and a heavy bag. When I arrived at the top, the look on the ERT guys faces was troubling. I asked the shift leader what was going on.

"I'm not sure, sir. We were all downstairs when we heard a lot of noise up here. No one came through the door so we didn't know what was going on." He went on, "He's been going at it a while. I think he hurt his hand hitting the wall."

"Is he armed?" I asked.

"As far as we can tell, no."

"OK good, let's back everyone up. Keep one armed individual up here with me and, here, take my weapon as well. The rest of the team can stay around to assist, but I want them to drop their weapons, and I don't want him to see anyone. No need to make him feel threatened."

"Roger that, sir," the shift leader acknowledged as I handed him my Glock 17.

The likelihood of having to get physical with the colonel was high, based on what I observed when I took a peek inside the gym. I didn't want to have a weapon on me and risk an accidental discharge, or if I rolled on the ground with him, I didn't want him to get ahold of it. I knew the colonel carried a sidearm, just like the rest of us, so I wanted to make sure a couple of the ERT guys were armed, just in case.

I stepped into the room and observed the colonel yelling. His face was red and he was foaming at the mouth.

"You! You don't want this!" He yelled at the wall.

"Colonel Lewis..." I said. He turned to me. I could see the drool. He began to walk towards me in a slow but steady stupor with a look of determination on his face—indicating that he may charge. I postured to brace in case he charged me. As he neared me, I said, "Colonel Lewis, don't come closer."

He stopped and stood straight up. "Oh, hey Cody. I didn't know it was you." He said as he squinted his eyes. The colonel didn't have any eyesight issues that I knew of, so it was clear he was hammered.

"What's going on, sir?" I asked.

"I'm just...I'm just here. Just getting a workout."

I kind of laughed. "Sir, it looks like you're getting more than a workout." He smirked at me and turned around to walk away. Suddenly, he turned around quickly and started to walk aggressively towards me again. I braced to receive him with both my hands up, and he stopped about six feet in front of me.

"Come on, Cody, fight me." He laughed and taunted.

"Sir, I don't want to fight you. I just want you to relax," I said.

"Come on," he said as he walked away. "Just fight me!" He said while turning around sharply again.

"Sir, I don't want to fight you. I wanna know what's going on. You wanna tell me?"

"Pfft, Cody, you don't know. You weren't there!" he yelled.

"You're right, sir. I don't know. That's why I'm asking you." I continued to try to deescalate the situation. Then he turned again and put his fists up. He started slowly walking towards me.

"Come on, fight me!"

"Hey, sir, you wanna fight? If you come closer, that's what's gonna happen," I said. "You need to stop where you are."

He laughed. "I'm just playing, Cody. Come on, you're big. You're a big dude." He kept laughing. "I like you, Cody. I like you" he said as he walked away again.

"Sir, the DPO is next door, and he called complaining about the noise," I said. The DPO is the Deputy Principal Officer, also known as the Deputy Consul General: the second highest-ranking U.S. Diplomat in Erbil.

"Fuck the DPO," the colonel said.

Again, I kind of laughed. "Right, sir. I agree. Fuck the DPO. But we still need you to keep it down."

This went on for about an hour as the colonel charged, yelled, and cried repeatedly. Slowly, I started to piece together why he was acting this way. The colonel told a story about a mission he conducted during a combat tour in Iraq several years before. His friend, also his Company First Sergeant, was gruesomely killed while fighting near the Euphrates river. The colonel gave descriptive accounts of the raid but in pieces, so I had to put it all together.

I also learned that earlier during the day when he was visiting the embassy in Baghdad, he met a soldier that possessed the same last name as his friend that was killed. They were introduced and the colonel learned, or already knew, that this young soldier was his deceased friend's son. He told me how he had trouble keeping it together when he met the soldier.

"Cody, I watched him die! I watched him burn, and I couldn't do anything," he cried.

"I met his son. I didn't know what to say. I couldn't help his dad!"

My heart broke for the colonel. I sympathized with him. His struggle was so real and humanizing. It was clear he was devastated. I just let him talk. I listened. I tried to calm him down as best possible. But each time he started to become more reasonable, within minutes, he'd become volatile again.

I called the new DRSO Harper and let him know what was going on. Within minutes, he arrived and I gave him the scoop.

"How long has this been going on?" Harper asked.

"Boss, I've been out here at least an hour, and the guys didn't call me right away."

"OK, is he armed?"

"Negative, he's unarmed, but he's been pretty aggressive."

"What did he drink?"

"The guys say he was pounding glasses of Johnny Walker at the wedding."

"Damn. OK, let's talk to him."

Harper stepped in to speak to the colonel, and I followed. "Colonel Lewis, what's going on man?" Harper asked.

"Harper! Come on, let's fight," he said as he approached.

"Colonel, I'm not gonna fight you," Harper said.

"Come on, it's fun. Let's fight."

The DRSO laughed again and brushed it off. This went on for about another thirty minutes. Finally Harper and I stepped out to talk.

"The ERT has an extra room downstairs. We can set a bed up for him and have him rest there. A medic can check up on him regularly." I said.

"That sounds good. If we can convince him to come down with us and stay here."

"Yeah. True. It's worth a shot."

Harper and I stepped back in and gently persuaded the colonel to come downstairs and get some rest. We told him about the extra room in the ERT house, and he conceded that he'd stay there for the night. I asked him where his weapon was, and he calmly explained it was on the nightstand near his bed in his house. I sent someone to his house to secure it, so that if he somehow left in the night, he wouldn't have access to it.

The colonel was exhausted. He slowly walked down the stairs to the spare room and began to take his shoes off.

I directed the medic to keep an eye on him, then I started to head back home. As I was walking away, someone yelled, "Sir, he wants to leave." I went back over, the colonel was much more relaxed as he was likely running out of juice and sobering up from punching the wall the past few hours. "I'm good, guys, I'm good," he said. "I'm just gonna go back to my place."

Harper and I discussed our options. "We can't keep him here against his will," Harper said. We decided to allow him to go back to his house but under escort. He obliged, so the colonel, Harper, and I walked back across the compound to his house. We told the colonel that we were worried about him, so we wanted someone to stay in his house. Although he vehemently denied needing anyone to stay with him, eventually he gave in and accepted our offer. Two ERT guys were going to stay in his living area to keep an eye on him.

I departed again, and just as I was arriving to my place, I got a call.

"Hey sir, we heard some rustling in the colonel's room. Now he's sitting in the living room in PT gear about to go on a run," the voice said.

"A run? It's 0330!" I heard laughter on the other end.

"Yes, sir. A run. He's beginning to stretch."

I walked back over to the colonel's house. Harper got the call too, and we met outside on his porch area. Harper tried to convince Colonel Lewis not to go on a run to no avail, but the colonel insisted.

At 0330, I sure wasn't planning on running with him, so we utilized some creative thinking and "strategery" and posted guys up around the compound on his path. Each of us could see the other, and we could see the colonel as he ran. Soon I noticed the colonel running at a good clip, and one of the ERT guys running with him in 5.11 cargo pants and boots! It was pretty impressive. I told the guy he didn't need to do that, but he continued anyway.

Colonel Lewis ran for thirty minutes or so until finally retiring to his villa. Our guys were still in his living area and would stay with him throughout the evening. It was shitty duty, but we needed someone to watch him.

The next morning Harper and I were awake before the colonel. I called over to the guys at his house and learned that he was still asleep. Harper and I strategized, determining our next steps. Unfortunately, too many people witnessed this event not take some sort of action. The colonel was a good dude, but if we did nothing, that would set a poor example and bad precedent for future incidents like this. We'd also be risking our own jobs.

Harper scheduled a meeting with the CG and the medical doctor. The CG agreed; we needed to take action. The CG directed Harper to contact the colonel's superiors in Baghdad while the medical doctor set up appointments at the Combat Support Hospital (CSH) that was located at the airport.

Harper called the general in charge of OSC-I in Baghdad and relayed the information. Harper tried to paint the colonel in the best light possible. The colonel had no record of misbehavior, and was a good contributor to the consulate. The general listened and assured Harper that he'd take it easy on the decorated soldier.

Later that morning, I escorted Colonel Lewis and the doctor to the CSH. He thought he was going there to get his hand checked since they had "better capabilities." The doctor, a quirky lady with the best of intentions, continued to tell the colonel that his hand would be looked at in a timely fashion. All the while, she was actually waiting to speak to the psychiatrist who was nowhere to be found.

While I waited with Colonel Lewis, we walked around a portion of the airfield that was leased to U.S. Special Ops. We checked out different aircrafts and talked to some of the staff that were lingering around. Colonel Lewis told me about his time in the Army, gave a more coherent version of his story from the previous night, and was profusely apologetic about what happened. I forgave the dude. It was clear he had an internal struggle he was dealing with.

Finally, we made it back from walking the airfield to the waiting area. The funny doc came out and said, "Almost ready! We're gonna get that hand fixed right up!" she said enthusiastically. I knew the doc was lying to him about getting his hand checked, but I was directed not to say anything. I didn't like this bullshit plan, and as time passed, I began to get more agitated.

Colonel Lewis knew something was up as well. He turned to me and said, "Cody, what's really going on?" I looked at him and couldn't hide it anymore, "Colonel, I'm gonna shoot you straight. This charade, it's all bullshit. Doc isn't here to have you get your hand checked out." We turned to look at Doc who seemed astonished that I'd break from character.

"The thing is, Colonel, last night was a big deal. Everyone heard you, including the DPO. We talked to the CG this morning, and he said you needed to come get checked out by a psych. He also said that Harper was to contact the general in Baghdad." The usually calm and considerate Colonel's face got red, a reminder of his rage from the previous night.

"Are you fucking kidding me, Cody? You guys have to tell them?" he asked.

"Sir, we have people we report to as well. We could get in a lot of shit if we sweep this under the rug."

"Fuck, thanks Cody," he said flippantly. "This is the end of my fucking career."

I didn't like that he was insinuating it was my fault, and I began to feel my patience waning.

"Sir, when we talked with the CG this morning, Harper highlighted that we wanted to minimize any negative impact on you." I said. "We had to follow his orders to contact the general in Baghdad."

"That's chicken shit, Cody. I'm not going to see the psych. You could have handled this differently. Take me back to the consulate."

I agreed to take him back to the consulate, but after a few minutes more of him blaming me for his problems, I had enough.

"This is fucking ridiculous, Cody" he said.

"You know what, sir, I didn't make you drink and act like an ass last night. You did. You had the whole fucking neighborhood awake with that nonsense. You're a grown-ass man. You wanna blame someone, take a good fucking look at yourself and own up to that shit." The colonel mumbled something under his breath, and we kept quiet the remainder of the ten-minute trip back to the consulate.

I arrived back to the consulate and briefed Harper on the colonel's objection to us notifying his superiors. Harper just shrugged his shoulders and said, "We had to do what we had to do. I didn't make him drink."

"Agreed, that's what I told him, but he's not buying it."

"It's the CG's decision, and it's final."

"Fuck it. We did what we could."

As evening came, I received several inquiries from the guys in my protective ops team about the colonel and the events the night before. They were wondering what was going to happen to him. They all respected and liked him. He treated them with dignity whereas many of the other diplomats did not. There was nothing I could tell them. I didn't know.

I crossed the colonel later that night while on the compound. He approached me and extended his hand, "Hey Cody, I'm sorry about earlier. I didn't mean to take it out on you."

"No worries, sir. It's been a rough 24 hours. What's the verdict?"

"The general is sending me back."

"Back where? To Baghdad?"

"Nope. Out of the country. He says I need help."

"Fuck, I'm sorry to hear that colonel. I was hoping he'd meet with you, and y'all could work it out."

"Yeah, me too. Fucking Air Force General though, what does he know." We both had an uncomfortable laugh.

"Anyway, I'm out of here tomorrow morning. Thanks for everything, and my apologies again."

"Roger that, sir. Best of luck to you."

"See ya, Cody."

Colonel Lewis was a good man. He was an excellent military officer and a fantastic leader. He treated all of my team members with respect. I liked him, and I hated to see it go down like this. We all just wished things had turned out differently.

Too often in RSO leadership roles difficult decisions like this have to be made. When it impacts a career or family life, it makes those decisions much more difficult. Harper and I discussed sweeping this "under the rug" and not telling superiors, but we just couldn't do it. Everyone on the block heard the colonel yelling. I wish things had turned out differently for the him. That final discussion was the last time I heard from him. I hope he is well, wherever he is today.

Chapter 12

DUCK AND COVER

One early evening in Erbil, I was stretching on the top floor of the gym on the northwest side of the consulate compound. Suddenly, out of nowhere, I heard a loud *boom*. I felt the walls shake around me as the shockwave from the blast nearly knocked me off my feet. The glass rattled and I could hear debris falling all around.

Immediately following the blast, I heard the duck and cover alarm sound over the consulate loudspeaker. The automated voice said "Duck and cover. Get away from the windows. Seek cover and await further instructions." In between those sentences was a piercing alarm sound, like the "hi-low" wail sound of your local police or fire department emergency vehicles. The alarm was not automatically initiated. The United States Marine on duty heard, felt, and saw the blast on his video monitor. He was quick to react and sound the alarm.

As I hurried down the stairs to the bottom of the gym, I approached two of my protective ops guys standing downstairs near the door. They were waiting and looking outside.

I yelled, "What are you doing?" as I approached them.

They responded, "Pausing, sir. Waiting to see if there is IDF."

I shouted, "That's long enough, bro! That's not IDF! Let's go!"

All three of us sprinted out of the gym heading to our respective locations to "kit up" with gear. We were stoked. Yells of excitement and laughter overcame us as we split ways to put on our gear. "Be safe, bud.

The sound of small arms fire from AK-47 Kalashnikov rifles continued popping off around us. As I ran down to my office on the south side of the compound, I noticed a large plume of dark black smoke to my left, just north of the east gate, right near the ten-story high abandoned hotel structure. That abandoned structure had direct line of sight into the compound. It was usually guarded by Asayish police officers. If the bad guys hit that building, the Asayish were dead. Furthermore, if they made it to the top of that building, they would have the high ground. That'd be a perilous situation for us on the consulate compound.

These were thoughts running through my head until my attention was broken by a flash— a friend of mine was running, how should I say, expeditiously. He was running faster than I'd ever seen a human move before. The bottom of his body was so fast that his torso couldn't keep up. It was Trey, dashing through the street running to take cover in his home. "Slow down, Trey! You're gonna hurt yourself!" I yelled. He didn't hear me.

After crossing through Trey's path of dust, I arrived at my office. I plugged the code into the door and headed for my desk to grab my gear. I saw my colleague, Allen, kitting up with gear at his desk. The look on his face was priceless as I walked through the door yelling, "Whooooo, let's go! Game time, mutha fucker!" I think he thought I was nuts. While we kitted up, I told him where the blast was, and that I thought the abandoned hotel was hit. "We need to get eyes on that hotel. We can't let them get the high ground," I said.

Within seconds, we sprinted out the door towards the ERT house. I told Allen to get with the ERT and head to the northwest vehicle gate. If they were gonna hit again, I suspected it would be through one of the vehicle gates. I proceeded to the northeast corner of the compound and took cover behind the 18-foot high cinder block T- walls in order to get a closer view of the hotel. I aimed my M-4 rifle at the hotel and looked through my ACOG sight. I didn't see any movement inside, only smoke billowing to the south side of it.

After a minute or so surveilling each floor of structure, I determined that, for the time being, no one was inside. I went back down the street of the ERT house and saw Allen getting in the vehicle. "Be safe, bud." He gave me a thumbs up. Oh and Allen, eatadik," I said; a commonly used phrase of endearment between Allen and I. The team then rolled out towards the northwest gate. The primary ERT had already deployed to the southeast vehicle gate; coverage was setting up nicely.

As I proceeded down the road towards the RSO office, I took a left at the T-intersection and made my way towards the east pedestrian gate. I saw a couple of our TC guys who were headed to take up position and stopped two of them.

"Hey fellas, we gotta keep eyes on that hotel!" I said, pointing at the abandoned structure.

"Grab that Suburban and angle it with the engine block shielding us from it."

"Copy!"

We were in an area with minimal cover, so we had to create our own behind the armored Suburban. The location of the Suburban also shielded us from the pedestrian gate, just south of where the explosion occurred.

As the armored Suburban moved into place, I noticed some of our overly motivated TC guys in a makeshift observation position directly above the blast site. I yelled to one of the guys on the ground just below them, "Hey, what the fuck are they doing up there?" He knew what I was thinking. "I don't know, sir. I'll get em down." Shaking my head but smiling on the inside; these guys were trying to get some of the action.

I began to call to defense positions on the radio to get their status, but radio communications were shit. I switched channels and tried to raise Tony to check his location, but no luck on that frequency either. I decided walking to each position was a better idea.

As I began to walk, I heard a barrage of gunfire on the rooftop to my left. Then the gunfire became more sustained. It sounded like the guys up there were in a firefight. I rushed over to the building where I heard the gunfire, and I ran up the stairs to get to the rooftop. This building had a pre-established observation post and fighting position on top. A 240B machine gun was assigned to it, but it didn't sound as if the 240 was popping off yet. As I reached the top of the stairs, I arrived to a door that opens up to the outside.

When I attempted to open the metal door at the top of the stairwell, it was apparent that it was stuck. I'd never had that issue with that door. The door was primarily made of metal, but in the center was several squares of small glass windows, maybe six to eight across. I gave the door a good shake, but it still stuck. It was knocked loose from the concussion of the blast, and now it just wouldn't open. I was in a rush to get to the guys on the rooftop. Frustrated, angry, and in a hurry, I punched through the glass. Rookie mistake. I reached around the other side of the door in an attempt to open it from the back. No luck.

As I pulled my hand back inside, I felt my black glove was wet as I noticed blood running down my wrist. When I had punched the glass, it penetrated my gloves and sliced one of the veins on the top of my hand. I didn't feel it, but it bled like hell. I put pressure on it to stop the bleeding as I stood there thinking what a shit show I now have on my hands. Gunfire still blazing on the rooftop, a fucking door that won't open, and now blood squirting into the air. I knew I was gonna get shit for this.

I reached for the first aid kit that was hanging on my gear when I heard someone running up the stairs. It was Jeff, one of the TC shift leaders. Jeff is a former 19th Group Special Forces Soldier, and an all-around great dude. He's also funny as hell. Jeff looked at my bleeding hand as I put pressure on it, stopping the blood, then releasing it as blood squirted out.

Jeff said, "What the hell happened?"

I promptly said, "I'm bleeding. Look. This ain't no fuckin bueno." As I lifted my finger off the wound. The blood squirted, I plugged it up again. "Dude, hook me up."

He let out a bellowing laugh and said, "But, what happened?"

"Mutha fucker!" I yelled, laughing as well. "The door wouldn't open, so I punched through the glass to try it from the outside," I said.

"I see it's still closed." He continued to laugh. "Why didn't you use your weapon to clear the glass?"

"Jeff, fuck, I don't know. Just hook me up, bro."

Jeff began to patch me up with my first aid kit. We laughed the whole two minutes while this was happening as he continued to talk shit. "That door kicked your ass, Cody!" He was busting my balls then and continued until I left Erbil...and still, to this day.

As Jeff and I were talking, another TC dude named "Ski" came the stairs.

"Oh shit, what happened?" he asked.

"Busted my hand punching through the window trying to get that door open," I said as I looked at the door.

"But why didn't you use your weapon?" he asked.

I just gave him a look and shook my head. "Incredible Hulk thought he could fight it," Jeff said.

As Jeff finished applying medical wrap to my hand, Ski, who was one of the largest dudes on the compound, tried to rip the door off the hinges. He gave it a good shot but no luck. He departed and said he'd find another way up. This was all in a matter of minutes, but by the time we were done, that particular onslaught of gunfire had pretty much stopped. Since it appeared there was no more action on the rooftop nor did I hear of any casualties or issues, I made my way out of the building and decided to go check the southeast vehicle gate where the primary ERT had set up.

I walked the compound past the restaurant named "Zimbas." I saw the fighting position on top of one of the rooftops on the corner house.

"Ya'll good up there?" I asked.

"Yes, sir, all good."

Cool. I then saw Brian who was the ERT shift leader on duty. Brian, a retired senior enlisted member of the U.S. Army Rangers, approached.

I asked him how things were going, and he gave me a quick brief of the ERT's set up.

Then I distinctly remember how good Brian smelled.

"Brian, why do you smell so fruity?"

"I was in the shower when the duck and cover alarm went off. Had to get clean for the fight," he said as we both laughed.

Brian was a hardass dude, getting him to laugh was uncommon, but he was in his element. He was down for a good fight.

I walked with Brian to the southeast vehicle gate to check the status of the guys at that post. This vehicle gate has a "man trap," a space between two large automatic gates. I asked Brian if anyone was in there, and he replied that there were men inside. I didn't like it. This was not Brian's doing. Those guys were ordered by someone else to keep the gates closed. That gate being closed meant that the people inside couldn't get out if it was hit with another Vehicle Borne Improvised Explosive Device, or VBIED, which we learned is what was used to attack the consulate and caused all this chaos.

As I approached the gate, Brian sent one of his team members, Scott, with me. "Hey Scott, take an angle on that gate but have some cover. The guards inside will be jumpy when we open it." I was concerned that when the heavy automated gate opened, that the Kurdish security guard on the inside would pop some rounds off. Scott assumed the "ready" position as he pointed his M-249 SAW on the corner of the gate. I knocked on the gate, and it slowly began to open. Scott moved with it to maintain his cover. A few Kurdish security guards walked out with an American member of TC.

"Hey bud, don't close this gate all the way. If you get hit, it'll be like a coffin. Leave a small crack where only a human can pass through, and you'll be good. It won't affect the security of these gates."

"Roger that, sir," he said.

I walked off saying goodbye to Brian and Scott and made my way between the buildings towards the safe haven.

The safe haven is where employees were supposed to evacuate to in this type of incident. It was in the react room near the Marines post. The react room is where all the Marines keep their gear so that, in an emergency, they can all respond to one place to get kitted up and take their positions.

As I entered the safe haven, I saw the RSO standing there with taking accountability of personnel. He looked goofy with his helmet crooked on his head.

I chuckled and asked, "Hey sir, everything good?"

"Still waiting on a few people to make their way over to the safe haven. Do you know where Dr. Suzy is?"

"Negative, sir. Probably in her house. Want me to check?"

"Yeah, go ahead and check," he said.

"Roger that," I said as I proceeded out.

I walked towards Dr. Suzy's house, and I finally ran into Tony.

"Dude, where have you been?!" I asked.

"Me? Where have you been?" in typical Tony fashion.

"Protecting freedom."

He let out a laugh, and said, "What's up?"

"Is Dr. Suzy in her place?"

"I guess so," he said, "let's go knock."

We approached the doctor's house and knocked.

"Dr. Suzy! It's Cody, open up!"

"Who?" she yelled.

"Cody and Tony," I said.

"How do I know?"

"Is there some type of code I'm not aware of?" I said to Tony.

"Because, uhhh, it is? Open up and you'll see." Tony and I were both laughing pretty hard at this time. Still, she didn't open.

"C'mon Doc! We need your help!"

Finally, after a couple minutes beating on the door and pleading, Dr. Suzy opened it. She was wearing her PPE and had a bag in her hand.

"Doc, we need you at the medical unit."

"Is everyone ok?" she asked.

"As far as I know, but it's still volatile outside the gates, so we need to be prepared. Come with us, we'll escort you."

"OK, let me grab some things." She stepped away to grab some items then returned.

"Where is the Suburban?"

"Suburban? What do you need a Suburban for?"

"I am not walking to the safe haven," she said admantly.

"Doc, it's just around the corner. My guys are busy."

"I'm not going if I don't have a Suburban."

Sigh. "OK, Doc. Standby."

I turned to Tony who had stepped a few feet away. "Hey Tony, have some of the guys bring the Suburban up."

"What? A Suburban? What for?"

"Yeah man, she won't walk. Just have someone drive it around, and we'll put her in."

"Roger that."

The Suburban rolled up, we put the doctor in it, and we walked alongside it around the corner.

By this time, we had probably been about an hour or so into the event. Random gunfire was still going off around the compound but much less frequently. I knew the night would go on much longer, and I needed to find my cell phone. It fell out of my gym short pockets as I began to run shortly after the initial blast. Tony and I started walking towards the gym area and toward the northwest gate to check on Allen.

As we walked, I asked, "We all good? Everyone doing OK?"

"Yeah, we're good. Only issue is if this goes on all night, we'll need a rotation and have to pull people off posts," he said.

Tony had a knack for management and leadership. As a former Staff Sgt. in the Marine Corps, he just got it.

"Roger that," I said. "We'll get to that when the time comes."

I arrived to the corner near the gym and looked down towards the northwest gate where I saw Allen.

"Yo! You good?" I yelled.

"Yeah, we're good down here!" Allen responded.

After checking with Allen, I searched the gym courtyard and finally found my phone laying in the grass. I picked it up and noticed about fifteen phone calls. Shit! I looked at the numbers, and it was the special ops guys. I called them back, and they picked up on the first ring.

"Cody, you guys OK? We've been waiting to hear from you."

"Yeah man, all good, but we could always use some help," I said.

"We're right up the road, but we can't get past the checkpoints that Asayish set up on your road. Can you let them know we're with you and get us in?"

"Roger. Standby, let me make a few calls," I said.

I notified Ali and he made calls to his contacts in Asayish to open up the checkpoints.

At this point, I was still in tactical gear but also in gym shorts. I needed to change. I told Tony I'd be right back and would meet him at the gate when the special ops guys rolled up.

The gunfire had subsided to almost nothing, but we still weren't sure what exactly was happening outside the gates. Reports of gunfire were reported at some of our positions on rooftops earlier, but luckily, no one was injured. We learned later that the gunfire was coming from the Asayish as they shot over the top of people's cars to keep them back. Seriously, no rules in Iraq. The problem is, when you shoot at a 45-degree angle over people's cars, rounds impact the higher buildings around the area. So, when we heard over on the radio a couple of times "I have incoming rounds" on such and such building, it was the damn Asayish shooting at us. It was unintentional but dangerous nonetheless.

Since the chaos had slowed, I figured now was a good time to put on some pants. I went to my building, and as I went to open my door, I realized my keys had fallen out also. I didn't see them near my phone. I pondered running back to get the keys then said, "Fuck it." After a few mule kicks, the kind where you stand backward and kick as hard as you can near the handle, the door split, and I was in. I remember thinking that the General Services Office would not be happy. Then I thought, who cares, we're under attack.

I quickly put pants on and went to the northwest gate. The special ops guys had arrived in three Toyota Hilux trucks. They were all wearing civilian clothes. As they got out of the vehicles, I shook their hands, thanked them for coming, and asked who the senior enlisted was.

"I am, Cody. What do y'all need help with?"

"We're all set now, but having more guns never hurts. We may need help with personnel later if we have to set up a rotation schedule for the guys."

Another guy chimed up, "Who is in charge here? I need to talk to whoever is in charge." He was the commanding officer of the team. No doubt an experienced dude, but I didn't like his tone.

I said, "Well, that depends. The Consul General is in charge overall. But in charge of security and this situation is the RSO. Which one do you wanna talk to?"

I'm not sure he liked my attitude.

"We need to cut the lights," he said. "How can we cut the lights?" he said as he looked up at the compound lighting.

"I don't know how to cut the lights, but you're gonna definitely have to run that by the RSO."

"Where is he?"

"He's in the safe haven taking his accountability of staff. His deputy is in the TOC." I pointed to the new TOC that was just behind him.

"I'll go inside the TOC," he said.

I called the DRSO to let him know that the special ops CO was coming in.

Tony and I walked away.

"Cut the fucking lights, bro?" I said to Tony.

He laughed. "Yeah man, that cat was intense."

"Fucking GI Joe."

Cutting the lights is a novel idea if we were getting sustained, or any, indirect fire or being blasted from the sky. But we weren't. Furthermore, this wasn't a battlefield. We were at the U.S. Consulate, a diplomatic facility, and the only "boom" we heard was the first one. I passed his stupid request to the RSO who looked at me like I was a unicorn.

The RSO shook off the question then told me that I needed to select a team to go outside to the blast site with the FBI liaison, Matt, so that could collect some evidence. We were going to be his protection detail.

By this time it was approximately 2000. I recruited my team members and headed out of the gate to the blast site. It was a mess. Just about everything in view was burnt. Pieces of cars were everywhere, and there was blood on the ground in some spots. I remember specifically Colonel Najat, the commander of the Zervany soldiers that worked for my unit came up to me with a rubber hose. It was the hose from the car. He kept trying to hand it to me. What was I gonna do with that? There were hundreds of people out here and thousands of pieces of evidence. I kept telling him to put it down. He was confused on my role at that particular moment. Generally, when I met with him on a quarterly-ish basis, I was one of the top guys on the totem pole as far as he was concerned. But that night, I was just another dude carrying a gun. He didn't understand the flexibility and versatility of my role and appeared dumbfounded that I didn't pay much attention to him. Keep in mind, at the blast site was every Kurdish cat that ever had any official contact with the

U.S. Consulate. They all meant well, but it was chaos. They were just in the way.

After about an hour, Matt concluded his collection of evidence, and we returned back into the compound. By this time it was assessed that security was set up sufficiently, and that the threat was mitigated for the time being. Everyone not on a security post went back to their offices, and the special ops team departed.

Several hours had gone by since the start of the attack. Dr. Suzy told me earlier that she wanted me to come by after seeing my hand wrapped up. I finally made it there and got my hand stitched up. As I waited to see her, I called my parent's home phone number from Dr. Suzy's office. My dad answered.

"Hey Pop."

"Hey Son. Are you OK?"

"Yeah, I'm good. So you heard about what is going on?"

"Yes, your mom called and told me. She was driving and heard it on the radio." He paused for a bit. I could sense his concern.

"Y'all gonna be OK, son?" I knew he wanted to ask more to learn if it was over. I couldn't tell him because I didn't know.

"We'll be fine, Pop. I can't talk long, just wanted to let you know I'm good. I will call again as soon as I can. Love you."

"OK, son, love you too."

My dad wasn't his usual self. Of course he was concerned, that was expected. In the past, I usually kept any type of danger I might be a secret from my parents. They didn't need to know. But since I called him, and mom heard it on the radio, maybe he thought this was more serious.

I later learned that my mother was driving when she heard the news on the radio. She told me, "My heart dropped. I had to pull off to the side of the road." After that conversation with Mom is when I began to give real credence to the idea of not coming back to Iraq. I had been three times: 27 months on the ground and my parents kept asking me not to come back.

Everyone knows it's rough on families when soldiers, Marines, and other service members go into harm's way. What members of our military go through is many times much worse than the VBIED we had experienced at the consulate. The significance of this event was magnified, however, because it was conducted against a U.S. diplomatic facility where we had no combat troops—just the agents, TC guys, some Marine guards, and local security staff to protect a compound full of untrained, unarmed American personnel. We were defensive in nature, not offensive. Sure, there were special ops guys in Erbil, but they weren't there to protect us. We were fortunate they came over to help. The airport had U.S. military on the ground, but they were all in support and logistics roles. Furthermore, Erbil was supposed to be the "safe" area of Iraq. All of these factors are the reason this hit national news so quickly.

After getting a few stitches in my hand, I went back to the office. All of the agents and a couple of the TC leadership guys came over so we could have a "hot wash," or an after action review. We all took our turns talking: what went right, what went wrong, and what we could have done better. The mood was pretty jovial, considering what events just took place.

Fortunately, everyone from our consulate staff survived. We only had a few injuries, mainly from those on the side of the compound where the blast took place. Unfortunately, though, not everyone on the streets came out OK. Three Kurdish citizens were killed and many others wounded, including one American teacher.[14] We were lucky. ISIS claimed responsibility for the attack. The intended target, we later learned, was in fact the U.S. consulate. We had no issues the remainder of the night.

I ended my tour in Erbil just about two months after this attack. It was a bittersweet feeling to leave. I had grown as an agent, as a leader, and as a person. I'd learned so much from those I served with. It was the most camaraderie I felt since leaving the Marines and Spartan 26. I longed for that type of bond, and I finally had it, even if just for a year.

Before I left, I was asked over to the TC management's house. I was told to swing by for a barbecue. Unfortunately, Tony wasn't there, but others, including Jeff, were. When I arrived, I noticed almost every TC dude was standing in the front yard. To my surprise, they presented me with a flag that was flown by the Marine Detachment over the Consulate in Erbil. Jeff and the guys said some heartwarming words about my service in Erbil. It meant a lot to me, especially coming from such an experienced group of dudes. It still brings me joy to remember that moment. The last thing he said was that I'd receive something in the mail, a plaque, that wasn't quite ready yet. "Roger that," I said.

A few months later when I was in home in San Diego, I received that plaque. It read: ARSO Cody Perron - Protective Operations - "Your window shattering approach to operations was breathtaking." - Task Order 13. At first I was happy to receive it, then confused. Then I realized the meaning and let out a big laugh. Dicks. I will never live that one down.

---

14 "Car bomb explodes outside U.S. Consulate in Iraq," https://www.cbsnews.com/news/car-bomb-explodes-outside-u-s-consulate-in-iraq/.

Agents Unknown

VBIED Outside the Consulate Gate.

VBIED Aftermath Outside the Consulate Walls

Striking a pose outside a blown out building on the compound.

Agents Unknown

Love note from the team.

CONCLUSION

When I first entered the DSS in 2008, my father had just suffered a heart attack. Fortunately, Dad survived, but I wanted to be near him during his recovery. I began to question myself and wondered if this was the right career path for me. I knew I'd be traveling frequently and living abroad. I'd certainly never be back to living in Louisiana. And the likelyhood of me being near him was slim. But when I told my Career Development Officer (CDO) about my dad's condition, he did everything he could to help. Before training, I was initially assigned to the New York Field Office. I asked my CDO if there was any way I could move closer to my ailing father. The CDO promptly assisted me, and DS made adjustments to send me to the Houston Field Office. I knew then I wanted to work for this organization.

My nine short years in DSS were some of the best of my life. I traveled to over forty countries, learned foreign languages, and was a part of history on several occasions. I developed invaluable skills and made some great friends along the way. The short stories depicted in this book are just a hand full of adventures I faced in my career. There are certainly more.

In Houston, as a brand new agent, I traveled to Honduras, Nigeria, South Africa, and Kyrgyzstan to protect Secretary of State Clinton. I traveled to New York City to the United Nations General Assembly to protect multiple foreign ministers. I protected the former President of Pakistan in Houston, and Israeli Defense Minister in New Orleans.

In Baghdad I protected inquisitive CODELs at the site where Saddam Hussein was hanged. I stood where the cameraman stood. Remember the video? I took other protectees to the courtroom where Saddam was prosecuted. I escorted CODELs to review prison facilities that held Al Qaeda fighters and former Baath Party Loyalists. I dodged IDF on a weekly basis, barbecued in 110 degree heat, and finally learned how to escape that dessert cart.

Ho Chi Minh City was one of my most rewarding assignments personally. While there, I was fortunate to travel all over Vietnam, learn the language, volunteer at orphanages, create the consulate boot camp, and fly in relic Vietnamese helicopters when visiting POW/MIA sites of downed U.S. pilots. I rode in a Vietnamese "speedboat" when I was a site advance for the visit of Secretary of State John Kerry during his visit to Ca Mau, Vietnam: the area he fought during the war. I visited historic sites in Hanoi, Da Nang, Nha Trang, Hoi An, and Dalat. I conducted one-on-one protection for Senator Patrick Leahy when he visited Da Nang. I facilitated the successful implementation of the Marine Security Guard Detachment in HCMC: the first Marine Detachment to return to Vietnam's south since their evacuation on April 30, 1975, during the Fall of Saigon.

In Erbil, I traveled by air and ground to the Syrian border. One time I took a sixteen-hour route along the Turkish border where I witnessed some of the most beautiful landscape I'd ever seen. I frequently visited refugee camps of Syrians where I saw despair at its greatest heights. I went to the town of Sulaymaniyah, just west of the border of Iran, and ate some of the best shawarma known to man. I interviewed ISIS hostages, facilitated the evacuation of consulate personnel, held ancient artifacts, and was able to lead men who helped me make real tangible changes in security programs that undoubtedly made us safer.

In San Diego I flew on a private jet when protecting Prince Andrew, second son of Queen Elizabeth and brother of the future King of England Prince Charles. I flew to Laos and Kenya as part of the advance security team to protect Secretary John Kerry. I finally had the opportunity to protect the Dalai Lama, and over the Christmas holidays of 2016, I flew to Hawaii and was part of the team to protect the Japanese Foreign Minister, Japanese President, and President Barack Obama.

Is that enough? There's certainly more. As DS agents, we too often take these experiences for granted. These adventures are just some that I recall, but they barely scratch the surface of what other DS agents have done too.

I enjoyed my time in the DSS. As I look back, I can say I got to do some pretty cool stuff. I have stories to tell my kids someday, and in some cases, I made a difference.

I always say that I've served with way more good dudes and gals in the DSS than I have bad ones. I've made some of my closest friends in this organization. I've been fortunate to, on most occasions, have some excellent leaders. I've never once regretted raising my hand to serve the United States, whether in the Marines, as a Diplomat, or as a Special Agent. Any opportunity to serve this country is an honor. I left with my head held high, excellent memories, and even better friendships. This isn't the last time I intend on serving my country, but for now, I'll hang my hat up and embrace the sweet civilian life. To my fellow agents, stay safe, and stay in touch.

    Thanks for reading.
    Cody

On a Vietnamese "speed boat" in the Ganh Hao River conducting Site Advances for Secretary of State John Kerry during his trip to Ca Mau, Vietnam.

Just before flying with the Consul General to visit POW/MIA sites in the South of Vietnam.

Hanging with the local children in Ca Mau, Vietnam. This may have been the first time they've ever seen an American.

Making bread with local Iraqi Kurds in Erbil.

Agents Unknown

Meeting with Colonel Najat, Commander of the Zervany Soldiers that worked in Protective Operations.

On a protection detail. Just riding around a golf course in New York with a sub-machine gun.

Agent in Charge of the Protection Detail for Prince Andrew in San Diego and San Francisco.

With Mom and Dad. Celebrating my return from Erbil.

BIBLIOGRAPHY

"Amphibious Ready Group And Marine Expeditionary Unit Overview." U.S. Marine Corps.
Accessed January 27, 2018.
http://www.marines.mil/Portals/59/Amphibious%20Ready%20Group%20And%20Marine%20Expeditionary%20Unit%20Overview.pdf.

"Apply for Nonimmigrant Visas to the U.S." USA.Gov. Accessed January 27, 2018.
https://www.usa.gov/visas#item-213289.

"Bureau of Diplomatic Security." U.S. Department of State. Accessed January 27, 2018.
https://www.state.gov/m/ds/.

CBS/AP. "Car bomb explodes outside U.S. Consulate in Iraq." CBS News. April 17, 2015.
Accessed January 27, 2018.
https://www.cbsnews.com/news/car-bomb-explodes-outside-u-s-consulate-in-iraq/.

Cooper, Helene, Mark Landler, and Alissa J. Rubin. "Obama Allows Limited Airstrikes on ISIS."
The New York Times. August 07, 2014. Accessed January 27, 2018.
https://www.nytimes.com/2014/08/08/world/middleeast/obama-weighs-military-strikes-to-aiD-trapped-iraqis-officials-say.html.

"Directory of Visa Categories." U.S. Department of State. Accessed January 27, 2018. https://travel.state.gov/content/travel/en/us-visas/visa-information-resources/all-visa-categoriEs.html.

"Former U.S. Consulate Official Sentenced to 64 Months in Prison for Receiving Over $3 Million in Bribes in Exchange for Visas." The United States Department of Justice. August 14, 2015. Accessed January 27, 2018. https://www.justice.gov/opa/pr/former-us-consulate-official-sentenced-64-months-prison-receiving-over-3-million-bribes.

Schmitt, Eric. "Commando Raids on ISIS Yield Vital Data in Shadowy War." The New York Times. June 25, 2017. Accessed January 27, 2018. https://www.nytimes.com/2017/06/25/world/middleeast/islamic-state-syria-raqqa-special-opeRations.html.

Smith, Kebharu H., and Suzanne Elmilady. "Prosecuting Marriage Fraud Conspiracies—Lifting the Veil of Sham Marriage." U.S. Department of Justice. November 2014. Accessed January 27, 2018. https://www.justice.gov/sites/default/files/usao/legacy/2014/11/14/usab6206.pdf.

"Treaties and Agreements." U.S. Department of State. March 07, 2012. Accessed January 27, 2018. https://www.state.gov/j/inl/rls/nrcrpt/2012/vol2/184110.htm.

"US hostage Kayla Mueller 'killed by IS', say ex-slaves." BBC News. September 10, 2015.
Accessed January 27, 2018. http://www.bbc.com/news/world-middle-east-34205911.

Wedeman, Ben. "ISIS devastated Mosul Museum, or did it?" CNN. March 13, 2017. Accessed January 27, 2018. http://www.cnn.com/2017/03/12/middleeast/mosul-museum-isis/index.html.

ABOUT THE AUTHOR

Cody Perron was born and raised in Ville Platte, Louisiana. He is a 1998 graduate of Sacred Heart High School. In October of 1998, Cody joined the United States Marine Corps and attended bootcamp in San Diego, CA. He then attended the Marine Corps School of Infantry where he graduated as the honor graduate. Cody served a total of 4 years and 9 months as a Marine before he ended his active service on 20 June 2003.

Cody then attended George Mason University (GMU) in Fairfax, VA. In 2006 he graduated from GMU with a Bachelor of Arts degree in Global Affairs focusing on Russia and Central Asia. He graduated with Cum Laude honors.

Two years after receiving his degree, he was accepted as a special agent with the U.S. Department of State, Diplomatic Security Service (DSS). He attended the Federal Law Enforcement Training Center (FLETC) in Glynco, GA, from September 2008 to December 2008. He continued his special agent training at the DSS training facility in Dunn Loring, VA. Cody graduated from special agent training in April 2009.

Upon graduation of special agent training Cody was assigned to the Houston Field Office (HFO); U.S. Embassy in Baghdad, Iraq; U.S. Consulate in Ho Chi Minh City, Vietnam; U.S. Consulate in Erbil, Iraq; and lastly, at the San Diego Resident Office (SDRO), where he resigned on 31 October 2017 to begin his life with his new family.

During his time as a DS agent Cody was the recipient of numerous awards including multiple Meritorious Honor and Superior Honor Awards.

Cody is currently the Co-Founder and Chief Operations Officer (COO) of Fidelis Global Group, LLC—a Global Security Services firm. Cody is finalizing his Masters Degree in Organizational Leadership from National University.

Cody enjoys spending time with his family, camping, hiking, snowboarding, and whitewater sports.

Made in the USA
San Bernardino, CA
22 May 2018